# REBUILD YOUR LIFE

## How to survive a crisis

## Dale E. Galloway

Tyndale House Publishers, Inc.   Wheaton, Illinois

First printing May 1981

All Scripture quotations are from the
King James Version of the Bible
unless otherwise noted.

*Rebuild Your Life* was originally published under
the title *Dream a New Dream.*
Library of Congress Catalog Card Number 79-92405
ISBN: 0-8423-5323-2, Trade Paper
ISBN: 0-8423-5322-4, Living Books edition
Copyright © 1975 by Dale E. Galloway.
All rights reserved.
Printed in the United States of America.

# Contents

# Foreword

One of the beautiful qualities about our God is that he always gives us a second chance.

This inspiring, positive possibility comes through strongly in Dale Galloway's honest and open sharing of his difficulties and his subsequent triumph in the power of God.

I know many people who are at the depth of despair will read this classical statement of hope and find a new birth of belief in the possibilities of the future. "If a minister could experience divorce and could rebuild a tremendous ministry for Christ—then I ought to be able to rebuild in my life too!" This will be the testimony of many people who read this book.

I have known Dale Galloway for some years now. I am excited to see how he is applying the principles of the Robert Schuller Institute for Successful Church Leadership in building a church in Portland, Oregon. Today's principles of possibility thinking work! They will help rebuild a life that has been broken. They will help turn a bleak future into a beautiful tomorrow.

I commend these words, in this volume, with the belief that God will have something to say to anybody who sincerely scans the spiritual message herein.

Robert H. Schuller

# Introduction

Having lost all sense of time, I wandered aimlessly along an unknown beach in the State of Washington. I was sobbing uncontrollably every step of the way. As the sun was going down and darkness was closing in, I dropped down on the beach completely exhausted. For me the sun had stopped shining; there was only darkness.

"Where the hell are you, God?" I shouted. Just a few brief months before, I would not have believed any true minister of God would think such words, let alone shout them angrily again and again at the top of his voice.

Anyone who has been broken apart emotionally by some shattering experience, be it the death of a loved one, financial disaster, a runaway son or daughter, a physical setback, or the most shattering of all emotional crises—divorce—knows what I mean when I say there was a pain inside me that cut like a knife. At thirty-one, my life was filled with success and all the things that I wanted most out of life. After two very successful pastorates, I was now pastor of one of the larger churches in our denomination in the State of Oregon. After I had been there only thirteen months, the church doubled in all areas, and was starting to fulfil some of the dreams that I had. I had a wife whom I loved and had been married to since our freshman days in college. If anyone had asked me just a few months earlier, I would have told them that we had a happy marriage. I had an eight-year-old son, who was my pride and joy and everything I could want in a boy, and a little girl five years of age, who had a way of wrapping her fingers around my heart.

Then came that fateful day in October when my wife told me that she did not love me, that she never had, and that she was going to take the children and leave me forever, moving 2,500 miles away to her hometown in Ohio. She announced to me that I was the loser and that I would lose everything. I would lose the privilege of pastoring a church I loved, I would lose the wife whom

I cherished and loved, and I would lose my two beautiful children. There would be nothing left for me.

In the following weeks and days I struggled desperately to try to save the sinking ship, all to no avail. Before ending up on that beach, at the bottom emotionally, I had gone four days without food, fasting and praying, calling on God to, by some miracle, save our marriage. Now, as I lay on the beach, I knew the marriage was over. My life as a minister would soon be wrecked. My children would be taken many miles away from me. Never before had we had a divorce in my immediate family and I didn't see how any of the family could ever accept me again.

My father, whom I loved and for whom I had great respect, had not only been a minister for as long as I could remember, but had for the past thirty years been the head administrator of our denomination in the State of Ohio. My dad's brother had also been a prominent minister. Both my grandfathers had helped to pioneer, and had literally sacrificed everything they had to help establish, the denomination that our family now enjoyed so very much. I grew up knowing how the church thought almost as well as I knew my own thoughts. Instinctively, I knew that there was no way that the people from this conservative, evangelical background would ever be able to understand my divorce. I would forever be, in their eyes, a "second-class citizen." In my brokenness and out of the anguish of my soul I cried, "Where the hell are you, God? Don't you care? Haven't I served you since I was fifteen years old? Haven't I tried to do everything that you have wanted me to do? I have never said 'no' to anything you wanted in my life. Where are you now? Don't you even care that I'm going down for the last time?"

After I had exhausted my frustration and anger by crying out so openly to God, I was finally quiet, and then I said, "God, my Father, I can't live without you. Forgive my rebellion. I place myself once again in your hands. Do with me whatever you want to do." It was in that moment of yielding, commitment, and resignation to God that the very Spirit of Christ came and ministered to me, saying "Lo, I am with you always, even to the end of the world." And I said, "Thank you, Jesus."

In the pages that follow, I will openly share with you out of my own life and out of the lives of many people whom I have had the privilege of counseling along the journey from brokenness to wholeness. The insight has come to me that no matter what the cause of one's emotional heartbreak, the pathway to healing and wholeness is much the same for each person. God has given universal principles for our emotional and spiritual healing. These principles of God have brought me from extreme brokenness to complete wholeness.

When a man hurts, God hurts with him. I firmly believe God is ready and eager to heal all brokenness and make any broken-hearted person whole again. Doctors tell us that when a broken bone heals, it is stronger in the spot where the break was than in any other part of the bone. So it is emotionally when one cooperates with God and seeks to be made whole; he will one day be stronger and better than he has ever been before in his life, equipped and ready to be used of God in ways that he could never have been used before.

For all those whose lives are broken, I dedicate this book to your healing. You, too, can triumph over emotional tragedy.

# 1

# Accept What You Cannot Change

The church sanctuary was beautifully decorated with mistletoe and holly, and a huge Christmas tree covered with gorgeous ornaments and twinkling lights stood in the corner. It was Christmas Sunday, 1970. From all over Portland our growing congregation had come together to celebrate the joyful occasion of our Lord's birth. If there was ever a man who loves to preach, it is me, and Christmas Sunday is one of my favorite Sundays of the year. Normally I would be at my best for a big Sunday like Christmas. In years to come I would look back on that Sunday morning, not remembering what I said, and wonder how I ever stood up, faced the people, and proclaimed the joys of Christmas on the saddest day of my life.

It all happened exactly as my wife had told me months before that it would. According to her preplanned time schedule, a total stranger handed me those dreadful divorce papers on that fateful Friday a few days before Christmas. Within twenty-four hours I stood at the Portland International Airport, and through misty eyes watched helplessly as the woman I had loved, honored, and cherished since I was eighteen years old led my two children onto an airplane and departed, never to return. Many times as a minister I have heard people talk like they thought there were some things worse than death. At that moment and in the following days, for me, life was worse than death.

What would I do? In less than twenty-four hours I was expected to preach the Christmas message to my congregation. I recalled a wonderful friend of mine whom I had admired when I was growing up and who I thought was a beautiful minister for God. Into his life came one of these shattering experiences. Ironically, it was just a couple of days before Christmas Sunday. Instead of standing up to the situation, he ran for dear life. He phoned my dad, who was the church administrator, late on Saturday night and told him that he was held up in a motel and wouldn't be at the church on Christmas Sunday. I remembered, as a young man, thinking what a shock that would be for the congregation, to come and find that their leader had, under pressure, fled the scene. Now I understood why he ran. At this time, I felt like running away and never coming back.

Several months before I had any knowledge of my impending, heartbreaking split-up, I had preached a sermon to my congregation, centering on the Prayer of Serenity. I shared with them how on many occasions in counseling, I had pointed people to this beautiful prayer, and that when people practiced it in their lives, it brought peace to their struggles. Little did I know how much I would soon desperately need this Prayer of Serenity:

> God grant me the serenity
> to accept the things I cannot change . . .
> courage to change the things I can . . .
> and wisdom to know the difference.

*Stand up and face the music.* I would have given anything in my power to avoid, to alter, to delay, to just stop that terrible day from coming. No one likes to hang out their dirty linen for the world to see, let alone a person who has been brought up to believe that the ministry should be far above the sins of humanity. I guess I would have been willing to have stayed home more nights, instead of spending so much of my time and energy away from home working with other people. I would have promised and tried to carry out anything she wanted if I could only have changed the nightmarish reality of that fateful day. I would have been willing to take all the blame. I was beginning to learn the first part of an important truth. There are some things that, try as you may, you cannot change. Whatever I might have done to avoid that moment was forever gone.

At the close of my sermon on that unforgettable Christmas Sunday, emotionally choked up and with difficulty, I announced to the congregation that I would like to meet them for a congregational meeting in the Fellowship Hall immediately following the service. The people jammed into the Fellowship Hall to see what the big deal was. I took a deep breath, stepped forward, and with God's help faced the music. I stated that my wife had chosen to leave, had filed for divorce, had taken the two children, and planned never to return. I asked them for forgiveness for my failure as a husband and to please pray for both parties at this time. People stood there in shock, not knowing what to say. I opened the floor up for questions, but, thank God, there weren't any.

> *Don't run from the things you can't change. Stand up to them. A man becomes bigger than the thing he stands up to.*

In the days ahead, I was to learn many more lessons about what I could not change. *There are things that cannot be changed, no matter how hard you struggle.* A few days later I stood at the bedside of a twenty-four-year-old, extremely intelligent woman who wanted so much to live and had everything to live for. Her ambition was to become a great trial lawyer, and she had the ability to achieve that goal. But now her body was stricken by a fatal disease. As we visited one day toward the end, she shared with me all her feelings concerning her fast-approaching death. She told how friends she tried to talk to would turn her off because they didn't want to talk about death. Detail by detail, she told me about the great struggle she had fought, how she felt cheated when the doctor said she would not live. She talked about all the things she wanted to do—to marry, to become a trial lawyer, to have children, to go places, do things, see things, and she told me how she had feared dying. I couldn't help but notice there was a serenity in her weakened voice. Finally, I asked her what the secret of her peace was. She will never know what she did for me when she shared that secret. Unknown to my friend, I was one of those confused strugglers. She said: "I have been at peace since that moment a few days ago when I accepted my coming death and placed myself in God's hands."

*The key to peace, inside, is to accept what you cannot change and leave it in Someone's hands who is bigger than you are.*

Many times I have watched people face through acceptance what looked to me to be impossible. "He is dead; I cannot bring him back." "She has left me; I cannot make her come back." Emotional healing begins as you take this first big step: Accept what you cannot change.

*What we accept we not only live with, but overcome.*

Recently I counseled a young woman whose husband had left her some time ago for another woman, with no desire to ever return, under any circumstances. Her doctor has tried to get her to accept this; friends have tried to get her to accept it. She refused to accept it. Consequently, she continues to be a broken, hurting person who cannot heal up.

Let's face it. There are some things you cannot change:

You cannot change the weather.

You cannot change the tick of the clock.

You cannot change the past.

You cannot change another person against his or her will.

You cannot change what is right and what is wrong.

You cannot change the march toward death on which a fatal disease takes the human body.

You cannot change the fact that a loved one has died.

*Get smart. Save energy. Stop the struggle. Simply accept what you cannot change.*

*Accepting means that you stop fighting the inevitable.* When those divorce papers were handed to me, there was a fight in me that wanted to go to court and contest the divorce for all I was worth. However, as the days passed, I began to ask myself some very important questions concerning how going to court and fighting would change anything or anyone's mind. I came to the conclusion that one cannot force another person to do something they do not choose to do. To openly fight it out in court would only compound the hurt. At this point, I asked God to help me to accept what I could not change. It was at this point of *acceptance* that my own emotional healing began. It was my first big step back from heartbreak.

> *I can change no other person by direct action. But when I change my attitudes and actions, people tend to change theirs in response to my change.*

*Acceptance stops a lot of hurt.* The most difficult thing I have ever done in my life was to come to the point of surrendering the right to be with my two children, to guide their lives, to enjoy watching them grow up, to have anything at all to say in their affairs. I decided very early in the divorce proceedings that no matter how it tore me apart or what it did to me emotionally, first of all I had to discipline myself not to do anything or say anything that would tear the children apart any more emotionally. I made myself a promise that under no circumstances would I say anything derogatory about the children's mother. Acceptance for me meant she would have the children in Ohio, and because of distance I would go months, sometimes years, without seeing my children face to face. After all these years I still have an ache inside when I think about being separated from Brian and Lynette. Yet, as I continue to accept this fact, they will live with their mother and I have no more right to them—responsibility, yes, but rights, no. My complete healing at this point is taking place.

On a Saturday, I drove over a hundred miles to Centralia, Washington, to visit a dear friend who is exactly my age. John Wright was my associate pastor for several years and just a prince of a Christian and a loving worker in the Lord's work. As much as he wanted to see his two children grow up, as much as he wanted to carry on a full life of ministry to accomplish things for Jesus Christ, he had to come to accept his impending death. Courageously, with great faith, and with expectation, he now awaited death, knowing that in God's plan, the best for him was yet to come. Three days after our visit together, my friend went to Heaven.

As I left after that last visit with John, his wife and I walked out into the front yard together. We talked about the Prayer of Serenity and Faye said, "For me, acceptance takes the struggle away." Whatever it is that you face, that you can't change—

give it to God. Stop struggling! The beautiful thing is that once we stop struggling, the confusion is all gone, the turmoil is over, and there is peace. The peace which passes understanding, which God gives generously to all those who accept what they cannot change. Accept. Then you, too, can have peace in the midst of the storm.

*Never worry about anything that is out of your power to change.* About ninety-five percent of what we worry and stew about are little things that we cannot change. When I first started our drive-in church ministry, I would worry every weekend about what the weather was going to be like. Was it going to rain? Was the sun going to shine? Unfortunately, or fortunately depending on which way you view it, it rains many weekends here in Oregon. Then I talked to Dr. Robert Schuller, pastor of a famous walk-in/drive-in church (Garden Grove Community Church) in southern California, and he gave me this wisdom: "Dale, if you are going to pastor a drive-in church, don't ever worry about the weather, because you can't change it. It's in God's hands." From that day to this, I have left the weather in God's hands. Whether it rains or shines doesn't make any difference to me. I have a great Sunday every Sunday.

> *Stop worrying over what you cannot change and enjoy living more!*

*There is no gain without pain.*[1] Out of my pain and agony came some needed changes in my personality. Shaken to my foundation by divorce, my eyes were opened to some things about myself that I didn't like. Speeding down the road to success in hot pursuit of my goals, I had not taken the time to be aware of everyday life, to enjoy the little things that make life fun. I was too busy *doing*, to *be*. People who knew me before and who know me now testify that out of my personal tragedy came changes for the better in my personality; now I am more fun to live with and life is so much more fun to live! Before, I did not have close friends. Now I enjoy many exceptionally close friendships.

I know people can change because I, for one, am not the person

---

[1]Robert Schuller, *You Can Become the Person You Want to Be* (New York: Hawthorn Books, Inc., 1973), p. 97.

I was yesterday. And with God's help I am going to keep improving and be an even better person tomorrow.

Stop trying to change that other person, and with God's help, change yourself. You, too, can change:

You can change your attitude.

You can change your personality.

You can change bad habits into good ones.

You can change your job.

You can change your marriage before it's too late.

You can change your brokenness into wholeness.

Every day people are changing, with God's help, into the beautiful people God created them to become.

> *Created for something greater than brokenness—*
> *that's you!*

How does one know the difference between what he can change and what he cannot? By communicating with God through prayer. From childhood I was taught to sing, "What a friend we have in Jesus."

> "Oh, what peace we often forfeit,
> Oh, what needless pain we bear,
> All because we do not carry,
> Everything to God in prayer." —Joseph Scriven

Commit—David says, "Commit thy way unto the Lord; trust also in him, and he shall bring it to pass" (Psalm 37:5). This big word *commit,* when practiced completely, gives one the wisdom to know what to change and what to accept.

The commit prayer goes beyond "You take it" to "I release it." There is quite a difference. It is the prayer I made that day, driving to Bend when I entered into a new level of Spirit-filled living.

In the early months of 1971, awaiting final court action on the divorce, I found that things that had never bothered me before were worrying me to death. And I was worried about the local church, and the effect my divorce was having on the congregation.

The date arrived for me to attend the State Ministers' Conference for our denomination, to be held in Bend, Oregon. The very thought of going and having to face my fellow pastors filled me with acute anxiety. I just knew I would be the subject of their conversations. That day, as the car was heading toward Bend, I practiced what I call "Let go and let God." I took my hands and cupped them in front of me, held them up, and verbally put inside those hands everything I was fretting over and didn't have any answers to. I said out loud as I held up both hands, "There it is, God; I can't change it, I don't know what to do with it, it's all so unacceptable to me. I have been struggling over it. I have been fighting it. I just don't know what to do. There it is, Lord, I give it all to you. I give to you what people think about me. I give to you what's going to happen to the local church. I give to you what's going to happen to my ministry." As I talked to God, I turned my hands upside down and said, "There it is, Lord. It's all yours." As I stretched my fingers out as far as I could, turning my hands upside down so that it was impossible to hold onto anything, as I dropped my arms to my side, a wonderful feeling of serenity suddenly spread throughout my entire being. I now had peace in the midst of the storm.

> *Let go and let God. Then you will know what to leave alone and what to change, and the result will be inner serenity.*

# 2

# Stop Playing the Blame Game

The Blame Game is one of those games we start playing before we even start to school. A three-year-old fell off his chair while the family was eating dinner. As he picked himself up off the floor, he gritted his teeth, slammed his fist on the seat of the chair as hard as he could, and exclaimed, "Dirty old chair, why did you make me fall off?" At three years of age, he was already playing the Blame Game. Children are not the only ones who play the Blame Game.

Like the young man who was kicking his car in the front end again and again, as hard as he could. His right front fender was dented in, and it appeared he had run off the road into a light pole. Now he was kicking the car, blaming it. Yes, people can be funny. However, the Blame Game certainly isn't humorous; it's a most destructive game.

Every time something goes wrong, it seems we humans want to fix the blame on someone or something. John 9 tells the story of Jesus' interaction with the man who had been blind from birth. At once the disciples demanded to know, "Who sinned, this man or his parents, that he was born blind?" In other words, they were asking Jesus, "Who's to blame?" Everyone knows you've got to blame someone—you've got to fix the blame! A man's a wino. The big question is, whose fault is it? Is it his own? Did his wife drive him to drink? Is it his parents' fault? A couple is getting a divorce. Immediately friends or anyone who hears about it, from the closest to the farthest away, start choosing up sides, playing the Blame Game.

Although the Blame Game is a popular game today, the Blame Game is an injurious game:

> It never heals—it always hurts.
> It never makes people whole in their relationships—it only breaks relationships.
> It never unites—it only divides.
> It never builds—it only tears apart.
> It never solves a problem—it only compounds the problem.

Jesus came to stop the Blame Game. In response to his disciples who wanted to know who was to blame, who was at fault, Jesus said in essence, "Forget the blaming games. Ask instead, How can we help this man? Where does he go from here? How can we improve this situation? How can we make it new and better?" How glorious is the way of Jesus!

## STOP BLAMING GOD

A father, in his grief over the death of his sixteen-year-old son, was blaming God. His son's life had been snuffed out in a mutilating automobile accident that was the result of a drunken driver going through a red light and hitting the car in which the boy was riding. To this father, in love, I said, "My friend, there are some facts that you should know:

"Rain falls on the just and on the unjust.

"It's not how long one lives, but how he lives. It's the quality of life that counts, and your son was a true Christian!

"There are certain physical and spiritual laws in the universe. There is a law of gravity. There is a law, for example, that if you go out on the highway and run down the wrong side of the road and hit someone, they will probably be hurt, perhaps killed.

"God does not cause tragedies to happen.

"This life is preparation; it is temporary. The best is yet to come.

"Many times in this world in which we live, things will be unjust and unfair, but one of these days God will straighten all of this out for all those who love him and are called according to his purposes (Romans 8:28).

"With God's help, you can triumph over this tragedy. Thank God that he is working in your behalf to bring good out of bad."

## *STOP BLAMING OTHERS*

To blame another person is to play God and judge—a task for which none of us is qualified. To blame others is all too often a cop-out, a cover-up for our own deficiencies that we are unwilling to admit and face.

Pete and Sharon sat across the desk from me in my office. This young wife of three years declared in the most bitter words, "I am absolutely convinced that he," and she pointed to her husband, "is cheating on me." I looked at her and smiled, trying to tone down the bitterness of her accusation. I said softly, "How do you know?" She replied sternly, "Because he has been stealing from his overtime pay. I know he has been stealing, and I demand to know what he has been doing with it!"

For the past several months this young lady had been holding this knowledge inside her and had allowed it to build up, until now it poured out in the form of an accusation. This resentment and suspicion had caused her to become very cold and frigid toward her husband.

Turning to Pete, I said, "How about this, Pete, have you made some extra money?" He said, "Yes." I said, "Well, what did you do with it?" Slowly he reached down into his pocket, pulled out his billfold, and replied, "It's all here." In fact, he took it out and threw it on the desk. Then he said, "I've been saving this for three months now so I could buy Sharon a special Christmas gift that I've been wanting her to have!"

Sharon had jumped to the wrong conclusion, had harbored bitterness for all these months, had played the Blame Game for all it was worth, and the results were a lot of wear and tear on her marriage. It was when the Blame Game stopped that understanding replaced misunderstanding.

In recent years, I've learned a magic formula for helping salvage shaky marriages. If just once I can get the individuals to stop playing the Blame Game—blaming the other person—and look at themselves and what it is that they have done wrong and what it is that they can do to improve the marriage, then they are going in the right direction. Next, if I can get them to admit their wrong in front of the other person and say, "I'm sorry," at that moment the relationship begins to mend.

*Man is never a failure until he blames someone else.*

*Blaming others is as old as Adam.* Adam explained his sin to God by saying, "The woman made me do it" (Genesis 3:12). Eve blamed the whole calamity on the serpent, "The serpent made me do it" (Genesis 3:13). To blame another is only to compound the wrong, not to take care of it. It seems the more wrong we are, the greater the temptation to try and blame someone else. It takes smart men and women to stand up to their mistakes and failings.

*When a man plays the Blame Game, it's a sure sign it's time for him to play the Confession Game and come clean with God—and be honest with himself.*

Beat the cover-up with confession—confession is good for what ails you. Stop the cover-up. It is no use; it will only increase your difficulty. There is only one healthy way to clear a guilty conscience, and that is the Christian way. Stop making excuses; face up to your wrongdoing. Openly confess to God, and forgiveness is immediately yours. "If we confess our sins, he is faithful and just to forgive us our sins, and to cleanse us from all unrighteousness" (1 John 1:9).

The bigger the man, the quicker he says, "I am sorry." In 1974, headlines on our sports page read: WOODEN SAYS, "BLAME ME." Coach John Wooden's UCLA basketball team had just had its incredible 88-game winning streak snapped in a 71-70 loss to Notre Dame. Looking back on the defeat, Wooden was at a loss to explain how the Bruins blew a big lead in the last three minutes. "With an eleven-point lead, it seemed inconceivable to me that we could lose it," he said. "Our teams are not usually criticized for their lack of poise, but if we did lose our poise, you blame me. We learned a lot which we will use next Saturday." Learn they did! They came back to win by more than twenty points over the same team. Before you can improve, you must admit your need.

*God asks of us what is good for us.* It is the frank acknowledgement of our own wrongdoings which opens the floodgates, and sends the water of life tumbling and rushing through the heart. Without full and honest confession, there is no peace, no banishing of the oppressive guilt which weighs the person down. Admit your faults—and be healed. Admit your sins—and be forgiven.

> *He who admits his failings is, in God's sight, anything but a failure!*

The story is told of a middle-aged lady who appeared to be the picture of contentment in the Bible study and sharing-prayer group in which she participated. Week after week, various members would share particular problems that they were having, and the group would respond and pray for them. This older lady would sit, week after week, not saying anything about herself personally. Then one week, the dam broke wide open; she opened herself up for help. She told how unhappy she and her husband had been for years, how there was a wall of coldness and hostility between them. And then her eyes lit up, as if for the first time she saw what their problem was. She said, "Oh, no! Oh, no! All these years I have been blaming him, when it was all my fault."

This lady went on to share with her Christian friends how incidents as much as twenty years earlier had made her refuse to minister to her husband. For these many years, she had blamed him for his coldness and lack of affection, for the wall that was between them. Now she asked the group to pray for her, and they did. She went home to confess her sin to her husband, and to ask him to forgive her.[1] "Confess your faults one to another, and pray one for another, that ye may be healed. The effectual fervent prayer of a righteous man availeth much" (James 5:16).

The following week, here came not only the woman but her husband with her, all smiles, arm in arm, like newlyweds. No one needed to ask what had happened. When she stopped playing the Blame Game, and confessed first to God, then to her husband, it opened the door for a new love. The unhappy couple became a happy couple when they quit the Blame Game.

> *I'm not responsible for the attitudes and actions of the other person, but I am responsible for my own attitudes and actions.*

[1]Adapted from *Habitation of Dragons* by Keith Miller (Waco, Texas: Word Books, 1970), pp. 131, 132. Used by permission.

*When you are wrong, admit it. When you are right, don't rub it in!* All too often we do just the opposite. We want to prove who is right and who is wrong; we're the right guy and the other guy is wrong. This kind of battle of the will has yet to build one relationship. Fighting over who is right and who is wrong tears: it tears down the other person, it tears apart the relationship, it tears up the person who does it. Save yourself a lot of grief, and make it a point to never point out another person's sins, and never point out where you are right and they are wrong.

*Confess no one else's sin but your own.*

## STOP BLAMING YOURSELF

*Good news! Jesus was nailed to a cross so that you could stop nailing yourself to a cross.*

For months I had been going over and over the same ground, admitting, confessing, looking at my failings, trying to see where I had gone wrong. All of the failures of a broken marriage were weighing me down. As I was driving down the freeway on a cold day in February 1971, I saw Jesus hanging on a cross, crying out these words, "My God, my God, why hast thou forsaken me?" There are no more despairing words than these. These words came from a broken man. Then the healing truth hit me. Jesus took all my punishments when he died on that cross. "But he was wounded for our transgressions, he was bruised for our iniquities: the chastisement of our peace was upon him; and with his stripes we are healed" (Isaiah 53:5).

When Jesus died on that cross, he took *my failures, my sins, my shortcomings, the punishment I deserve*. I saw that to go on punishing myself and beating myself down for something that I had done wrong or failed to do right, was to fail to accept what Jesus did for me when he took my place on the cross. Then God gave me this freeing verse, "There is therefore no condemnation to them which are in Christ Jesus" (Romans 8:1).

Alice was condemning herself over the last words that she had spoken before her husband left the house and was killed in an accident. I said to Alice, "Stop it! It's inhuman to keep inflicting yourself with this mental torture over this past mistake. You've asked God to forgive you and he does. It is against God's will to go on punishing yourself." Forgive yourself. It's the only decent thing to do.

Too many people become their own judge, jury and prosecutor, continuing to inflict blow upon blow of self-condemnation on themselves. Nothing drags down one's self-love more than the depressing recall of shameful deeds or failures. It serves no good to keep going over past mistakes. It is a burden too large for any one person to bear. It will result in mental strain, nervousness, and acute anxiety. It will destroy your confidence. Believe that Christ Jesus took upon himself all your punishment when he died upon the cross. Accept it, and be thankful.

*Jesus was hung up for our hang-ups.*

Although it may be difficult to keep self-despairing memories from coming to mind, you don't have to give them a hearty welcome! You don't have to throw the door wide open! Shut the door in their face by saying, "God has taken care of it."

*God has forgiven you, now forgive yourself!* Exonerate yourself for the unwise decisions you made, for the selfish things you have said, for the times you let yourself down, for times you let your friends down. Let Christ erase the shame over any and all failures in your life.

Affirm right now this truth: Christ lives within me—so I am a wonderful person. Christ has forgiven me—so I will forgive myself. Stand up straight and tall. Face the sun. You're not the same person today that you were yesterday. Thank you, Jesus, for complete forgiveness!

Jesus said, "Neither do I condemn you. Go and sin no more."

Jesus says, "I forgive you. Go and play the Blame Game no more."

*A man is never more right than when he refuses to play the Blame Game.*

# 3

# Make the Wonderful Discovery of Who You Are

Suddenly there was a lot of confusion about who I was. Since the night I preached my first sermon at age seventeen, I had enjoyed much respect from many people. Now in the middle of a divorce suit, I had lost most of that respect I had enjoyed. There were a handful of ladies in my congregation who identified so closely with the divorcing wife that they were almost convinced that I was the devil himself. As I continued to preach from Sunday to Sunday, they would glare at me with hatred in their eyes, suspecting some sinister motive in every word I spoke. There were many wonderful people in the church I pastored who were loving and kind; yet the vibrations told me that their confidence in me as a spiritual leader had been severely damaged. No doubt this was due to their upbringing in the church as to "how sinful divorce is." I deeply appreciated their love and acceptance of me, yet their lack of confidence in me as spiritual leader shook my self-confidence.

Then there were those derogatory statements in the divorce papers which hit hard at how I had thought of myself as a good person. My life had been devoted to becoming the best minister possible, and now I had become a very poor example of those things I preached and taught. I thought, "Divorce—I must be a very bad person." Never had I felt "wormier" in my entire life!

"I'm all washed up." "I've had it." "I'll never amount to anything." "I'm a total wash-out." "I'm finished." "I'm down the tube." All of these statements characterized my feeling at the time.

Then I made a discovery—none of these statements was true. Every one of these statements was an exaggerated untruth!

The third step in my emotional healing was when I made the wonderful discovery of who I was—a son of God! You, too, can make this wonderful discovery. You were created for something greater than:

To be berated by a poor self-image.

To be sinking when you could be rising.

To be whimpering when you could be whistling.

To be hurting when you could be healed.

To be overcome when you could be overcoming.

*A new discovery of the wonderful person you really are awaits you—now!* I want you to discover, as I have, what a wonderful person you really are and can become, no matter what has happened in your life, no matter what you have done or failed to do or how you think of yourself at this moment.

In God's sight you are not:

A wash-out.

A complete failure.

A hopeless sinner.

> *God says that you are worth loving—so begin now to love yourself. God's greatest creation is—you!*

What a Creator God is! "The heavens declare the glory of God; and the firmament showeth his handiwork" (Psalm 19:1). Open your God-given eyes! The trademark of the Master Designer is upon everything in our universe. No wonder the songwriter declares of God, "How Great Thou Art"!

*Of all God's wondrous creations you are his greatest!* The finest; the most wonderful; the choicest; the *best!* God has made you "a little lower than the angels, and hast crowned (you) with glory and honor." He made you "to have dominion over the works of (his) hands" (Psalm 8:5, 6).

*A divine original—that's you.*

Someone special—that's you. God made you unique. There is no one else just like you. In the master planning of God himself, every man is created with many things in common. Yet each is distinct, and different from any other human being. No two snowflakes are identical. Each blade of grass is different from all others. How much greater are you than a snowflake, than a blade of grass. Of all the billions of people created, there is no one else who has ever lived or who is alive now that is just like you. You are a divine original.

Sam is fifty-six years of age, and throughout his life he has hated himself. Sometimes mildly, sometimes severely. Why? Listen as he sits in his pastor's study and pours out his story. "All my life," Sam said, "I have tried to be somebody else and I've been miserable. I never dared to be myself. I didn't think I was good enough, so I've been a phony for over half a century." That's the trouble with so many of us, we're always trying to be someone else and that's impossible: God never intended for you to be another person. He made you to be yourself. Do yourself a favor, be yourself.

*Accept this fact: You are not inferior to anyone.* Different, yes, wonderfully different. Wouldn't it be a dull world if we were all just alike. Never forget that you are God's idea—and God only dreams up fantastic ideas.

One of the worst crimes you can commit against yourself is to play the Comparison Game. Don't do it—don't compare yourself with another person. It is not God's best for you; it is an unhealthy thing to do. We need to get it through our heads that we were never made to be like any other person. Accept yourself for who you are, and with God's help become that wonderful person he created you to be. Refuse to play the Comparison Game and be a healthier, happier person.

*God loves you!*

The boy who held his little boat and said, "It's mine, I made it," suffered a keen disappointment. One day, with exuberant anticipation, he carried his boat to the shore of the lake and sailed it on the clear, blue water. The little boat skimmed along as the gentle breeze blew its sails across the rippling waves. Then suddenly, a gust of wind caught the little boat and snapped the string the boy was holding. Out farther and farther the little boat sailed until at last it had vanished from sight. Sadly the boy made his way home—without his prized possession. It was lost.

The weeks and the months went by. Then one day as the boy passed a toy shop, something caught his attention. Could it be?

Was it really? He looked closer. It was. Yes, there in the display window was his own little boat. Overjoyed, the boy bolted into the store and told the owner about the boat on display. It really belonged to him. He had made it, hadn't he? "I'm sorry," the shopkeeper said, "but it's my boat now. If you want it, you'll have to pay the price for it."

Sad at heart, the boy left the store. But he was determined to get his boat back, even though it meant working and saving until he had enough money to pay for it.

At last the day came. Clutching his money in his fist, he walked into the shop and spread his hard-earned money on the counter top. "I've come back to buy my boat," the boy said. The clerk counted the money. It was enough. Reaching into the showcase, the storekeeper took the boat and handed it to the eager boy. The lad's face lit up with a smile of satisfaction as he held the little boat in his arms. "You're mine," he said, "twice mine. Mine because I made you, and now, mine because I bought you."

Not only did God make you, but in Christ he paid the price to buy you back. Why? Because God believes you are worth loving.

Two birds were flying through the morning breeze, when one said to the other, "Look down at all those humans fretting." To this the other bird replied, "You know, they must not have a Heavenly Father like you and me." Jesus said, "Look at the birds! They don't worry about what to eat—they don't need to sow or reap or store up food—for your heavenly Father feeds them. And you are far more valuable to him than they are" (Matthew 6:26).

God believes you are worth saving. "You mean even with my sins?" Yes! "Even with that which is degrading to look at about myself?" Yes! "With all my faults?" Yes! "With my shameful past?" Yes! God looks beyond everything that is wrong with us and sees the good, the great potential. God sent Jesus Christ to die on a cross to eliminate the bad, the degrading, the shameful—our sin—and to bring out the best in us. God believes in you. Jesus Christ died to restore your lost self-respect. To give you back dignity. To make you able to walk with your head up high. Wow! What a great love God has for you.

*Make this glorious realization yours: "God loves me."* When Karl Barth, one of the great theologians of this century, came to America in 1960 to lecture at a seminary in Chicago, people came from all over America to hear him. Just before the opening session in Chicago, a reporter asked Karl Barth, "Mr. Barth, what is the most profound thought you have ever had?" Without a moment's hesitation, Karl Barth answered, "The most profound thought I know is the one expressed in a children's song my mother taught me as a boy—'Jesus loves me, this I know, 'cause the Bible tells me so!' " What could be greater than to be loved by God?

> *God loves you. Who are you to not love what God loves?*

Three times during the last several months, Harriet had tried to take her own life. A friend had brought her to my office in desperation over her threats to do herself in. As I looked at Harriet, I saw the face of a depressed person who thought she had nothing to live for. She felt worthless, useless, unloved.

She talked for a long time. Then I said, "Now I've listened to you, will you listen to me for just a few moments?" She agreed. I looked into her face and said, "Harriet, God loves you. He's got something better for you than this." And when she looked like she didn't believe me, I continued. I told her about Jesus and what he did when he died on a cross for her, how he proved God's love for her. I said, "I want you to do something for me, I want you to say three words." She said, "It depends what they are." I said, "They're not hard to say, they're healing words. They're words that can change your self-condemnation to self-acceptance. Here they are: God loves me."

Resisting a little, she slowly said the three words. I said, "Say them again." Much easier this time, she said, "God loves me." I asked her to say them a third time and as she did, she smiled a little. She said, "This seems kind of silly." I said, "You want to have help, don't you, Harriet?" She said, "Yes, I need help." "Then make me this promise. For the next two days, every time you start to be depressed, I want you to say these three words: God loves me. Over and over again. Will you do that?" She promised me that she would.

Two days later Harriet called me on the phone, with some newfound excitement in her voice, and she said, "Pastor, it really works. God does love me! I feel like I have something to live for, I'm a loved person."

> *There is nothing more healing than to accept God's love.*

To you, God says:
My child, I love you.
My child, I accept you.
My child, I care about you.
My child, I forgive you.
My child, I'm going to use you.
My child, I am with you all the way.
So now, accept God's love and love yourself.

> *To love yourself is the Christian thing to do!*

To become like Jesus is to love what he loves—and he loves you.

Some people have the mistaken notion that it's wrong to have good feelings about oneself. How wrong they are! The truth is: It is a sin not to love what God loves. To love yourself is:
Not only the healthy thing to do,
Not only the decent thing to do,
Not only the way to be liberated from negative attitudes,
Not only freeing you to love others,
Not only respecting what God respects,
But—to love yourself is to do what Jesus told you to do.

He said: "Thou shall love thy neighbor as *thyself*." During the time when my self-image was really suffering from what people were saying about me, I picked up Dr. Robert Schuller's book *Move Ahead with Possibility Thinking*, which I had read several times. My eyes fell on these lifting words: "I'm really a wonderful person when Christ lives in me. I've been too self-critical. I've been my own worst enemy. I'm a child of God. God loves me. I can do all things through Christ who strengthens me."[1]

As I finished reading these wonderful words, I bowed my head and said, "Thank you, Jesus, because you love me. I am a child of God." In those moments, a great sense of newness and a sense of being a worthwhile person, loved by God, flooded my mind. You, too, can let God give your self-image a new charge.

[1]Robert Schuller, *Move Ahead with Possibility Thinking* (Garden City, N.Y.: Doubleday & Co., Inc., 1967), p. 35.

*Only a worm was made to crawl and stay down.*
*Stand up and become God's man, God's woman*
*—love yourself.*

Who am I? I am the greatest person anyone could ever be—not because I am perfect, but because I am a child of God! The Bible says, "As many as received him, to them gave he power to become the sons of God, even to them that believe on his name" (John 1:12). The minute one receives Jesus Christ as Lord and Savior, he is immediately adopted into the family of God. Right then Jesus gives that person the name Christian, with a lifetime to grow into that name. There is no one reading this book who can't become a child of God this moment. Open your heart's door, let Jesus come in. If you are not a child of God, it is for only one reason. You haven't yet accepted your rightful sonship that Jesus came to give you. Every child of God belongs to the royal family.

*What could be greater than to be a child of God?*
*Thank you, Jesus—I am your child.*

In ancient architecture, there was no building that excelled the breathtaking splendor of the Temple which Solomon built for God. It was magnificent! It has been estimated, based on present-day construction costs, that it would cost more than the debt of World War II to build. Nothing was spared in its construction.

In the Old Testament, a great to-do was made over the building of the Temple in Jerusalem. Its magnitude and magnificence has not often been matched in history. It was the Holy Place where God's presence dwelt. Unbelievable, yet true, is this fact! Now, since Jesus has come, we are to be the "temples of God" (1 Corinthians 3:16). Think of it! You are to be the "temple of God." The living, breathing being in which God dwells.

At an early age I was taught that being the "temple of God" meant there were things I should not do to my body. This is true. However, in recent years I have discovered an even greater truth about what it means to be the "temple of God." If I am the temple of God, where God dwells, then I am even more magnificent and of far more beauty than the great Temple Solomon built. *Yes, you were created for something great—to be the temple of God* (1 Corinthians 6:19).

*Created to be the temple of God–that's you!*

I entered a house where there was little or no furniture, some boxes sitting around, books of pornography on the floor. There for the first time I met Darrel, who had just tried to commit suicide two days before and was on the verge of another attempt. He said, "I am worthless, I do not deserve to live." I looked into the face of a broken man, into eyes filled with pain and said, "My friend, God created you for something better than this." I shared with him the exciting truth of how he was to be the temple of God.

Six months later in a Pastor's Class, the same Darrel prayed this prayer: "I thank you, God, that I am your temple, because you love me and think I'm a worthwhile person. I now want to live. I am learning for the first time to love myself. Thank you, Jesus! Amen."

*Not perfect–but becoming.* So many people suffer from a sense of unworthiness because their lives do not measure up to their ideals. The emotional cost of being unwilling to accept anything unless it is perfect is very high. If you have strong tendencies toward being a perfectionist, you need to admit it. Then you need to accept the fact that no one except Jesus Christ himself has ever been perfect in performance. Having the love of God in life is not conditional upon your doing everything perfectly. You don't have to prove anything to God, he accepts you as you are. He says to you, "Let's go from here to become the wonderful person I created you to be."

Dr. Allen, pastor of one of the largest Methodist churches in the world, tells this story: "An outcast beggar was sitting across the street from an artist's studio. The artist saw him and quickly began to paint his portrait. When it was finished, he called the beggar over to look at it. At first the beggar did not recognize himself. 'Who is it?' he kept asking. The artist smiled and said nothing. The beggar kept looking at the portrait until recognition began to dawn. Hesitantly he asked, 'Is it me? Can it be me?' The artist replied, 'That is the man I see in you.' Then the beggar made a wonderful reply, 'If that's the man you see, that's the man I'll be.' "[2]

---

[2]From *Life More Abundant* by Charles L. Allen (Old Tappan, N.J.: Fleming H. Revell Company). Used by permission.

*You can become that beautiful person God created
you to be.*

You are to be used of God to do wonderful things. Jesus said:
"You're the salt of the earth . . . the light of the world." Life for you
is not over, you are not washed up, you are not too old. You have
not made too many mistakes.

David commited the sins of adultery, murder and cover-up.
When he repented and came clean with God, God loved him and
used him. God will use you. Believe it!

*There is no greater thing than to be used of God.*

Everybody thought I was all washed up as a minister. A personal
friend, one of the highest officials in the denomination in which I
pastored, told me straight out that I would have to leave the
pastoral ministry. According to this church official, pastoring for
me was over; because of divorce I was forever unfit. Something
inside of me did not believe it. I could not believe God wanted me
to be put on the shelf. The unstoppable desire of my heart is
expressed in the chorus "To Be Used of God," by Audrey Mieir.[3]

> . . . To sing, to speak, to pray,
> To be used of God to show someone the way;
> I long so much to feel the touch of his consuming fire.
> To be used of God is my desire.

If there is anything I have found that God honors, it is desire.
When I was at my lowest emotionally, I never lost my desire to do
God's work; more than anything else, I wanted to serve God. My
greatest joy is when God is using me. For the biggest self-image
boost there is: let God use you. Not next year, but now! Today
God is using me in greater ways than ever before. Who would
have believed God would use a divorced minister to build a great
church "for the unchurched thousands"? I thank God that he's not
finished with me yet.

Friend, neither is God finished with you—the best is yet to
come.

---

[3]From "To Be Used of God" by Audrey Mieir, ©1974 by Manna Music, Inc. 2111
Ken Mere Avenue. Burbank, California. Used by permission. All rights reserved.

**4**

# Slam the Door on Self-pity

"Nobody loves me, everybody hates me, I think I'll eat some worms." So goes the funny little song I used to sing as a boy; but now I wasn't jesting. This song expressed how I felt. I had lost my wife, I had lost my children; now it appeared I was fast losing my church. I reasoned, "People are talking about me; nobody understands what I am going through. I don't deserve this. People don't care what's happening to me. No one ever had it any worse." I had allowed private enemy number one—self-pity—to seize control of my mind.

True, self-pity may not make you eat worms, but it surely can make you feel wormy.

*Watch out for private enemy number one–self-pity.*

Self-pity is an all too familiar mood. Elijah, one of the greatest prophets who ever lived, is pictured in Old Testament Scripture sitting under the juniper tree singing the blues, having allowed self-pity to overtake him. Peter, one of the greatest disciples who ever lived, is pictured in the New Testament as sitting by the Sea of Tiberias feeling sorry for himself because God has laid on him the sacrificial responsibilities of doing Kingdom work. Psalm 73 is about a man who was pitying himself because the wicked were prospering and he was having a hard time. How up-to-date the Bible is! Self-pity not only plagued people who lived yesterday, but is constantly trying to get control of our minds today. Although

**35**

self-pity has been around since the beginning of time, it never has done one person any good, and it never will.

*Self-pity is an ever-present temptation to those who are going through an emotionally shattering experience.* When a loved one has died, when you've lost a job, when you face financial disaster, when your marriage is falling apart, when your children have run away from home, when the doctor has told you that you have an incurable disease, in a time of personal catastrophe—look out for self-pity. Believe it or not, self-pity can do you far more harm than the things that happen to you. Now, we cannot do anything about a lot of the things that happen to us, but we can do something about self-pity. You do not have to put up with self-pity. You can do something about it—you can get rid of self-pity.

*Self-pity is the one luxury that no man can afford.*

*One certainly does not rebuild his sense of self-worth by indulging himself in self-pity.* Self-pity does not generate self-respect, it wipes it out. Self-pity does not free one from the unhappy past, but enslaves one to his past. Self-pity makes one live in that past, instead of bravely facing the present. Self-pity is demoralizing. In short, self-pity is self-destruction. So don't do it. Don't harm yourself this way.

> *To engage in self-pity is to hurt yourself far more than anything that has happened to you can hurt you.*

A year ago a very good friend of mine, Bryce, was one of the largest home builders in the State of Oregon. At one time he had 175 homes under construction. Bryce and his family worked hard to build a successful home building business. Being a success-oriented person, one of my friend's dreams was to be *the* largest builder of homes in the State of Oregon. He was right on the threshold of the fulfillment of that dream when the money market changed, prices went sky high, interest rates accelerated. Bryce got caught in a financial squeeze. Having enough assets to cover liabilities but not enough cash flow to meet current obligations, he found himself in the middle of financial heartbreak.

A depression settled down heavily on my friend's life. He was depressed when he went to bed, and depressed when he got up in the morning. Everywhere he went throughout the day, depression went with him. Bryce, being the championship person that he is, determined to beat the depression; but before he could beat it, he had to discover the cause.

My friend discovered what was making him so depressed. Surprisingly enough, it was not the catastrophes that were happening to him daily, it was not that his business had collapsed, it was not even that he didn't know how he was going to support his family and six children. Do you know what was the cause of his depression? He told me that he came to realize that the cause of his depression was self-pity. Once he acknowledged to himself what it was, he stood up to it and slammed the door on it. The depression left him. Slam the door on self-pity and you will rid yourself of depression.

> *Self-pity opens the door for depression. Close the*
> *door on self-pity and you shut out the major cause*
> *of depression.*

A year ago my father passed away. It wasn't very many days until my mother wanted to sell her house and move into an apartment. The next time I talked to her she wanted to do something else. Finally I said to her one day, "This emotional swing that you are experiencing is normal in view of what you've gone through. Do not make major decisions while you are in this mood swing unless you just have to." When one is going through an emotionally shattering experience, his moods change rapidly. He may decide to do a hundred different things the same day, many of which contradict each other. If this describes you at this time, just accept it as where you are emotionally. Relax in God's great love. He loves you right where you are. God's love is utterly patient, because God knows where everyone is on his earthly journey.

*Self-pity mars our relationship with others.* The man who is forever going over and over things that he regrets about himself will not long maintain his friendships. This is not too surprising, because a self-pitier is unattractive. People avoid the company of a person who is always complaining.

Over and over again, Linda recited the same old things like a broken record. After I had listened to her on several occasions, and she didn't want to follow my suggestions, I noticed that she sought out someone else to listen to the same old broken record.

Some people take delight in wallowing around in self-pity, but it is certainly never delightful to other people. My friend to whom Linda talked had a little more courage than I did, and he said to her, "Why don't you stop feeling sorry for yourself?" Do you know what? She did. She stopped, and within a few days her depression was gone. Soon she was smiling instead of having both sides of her lip hanging down.

> *Self-pity: The one attention-getter that soon wears out the other person's attention.*

*Self-pity stops your progress.* Allow self-pity to take over and all achievement comes to a standstill. When you are sitting on the sidelines doing nothing but feeling sorry for yourself, that's exactly what's happening—nothing. This is not the way to make your situation better. You want things to be better? Then get off your seat and do something about it.

> *Don't just sit there on the sidelines and feel sorry for yourself. Get up and get into the action.*

Ask yourself, Has self-pity ever done anything good for me?
Does it ever change what has happened? Never.
Does it ever make good come out of bad? Never.
Does it ever make you feel better? Never.
Does it ever make you feel loved? Never.
Does it ever build your self-love and respect? Never.
Does it help you achieve and accomplish? Never.
Does it bring you closer to others? Never.
Does it make you more loved by others? Never.
Does it bring you into a closer fellowship with the all-powerful One? Never.
Does it ever build your morale? Never.
Does self-pity ever help the wounded pride to heal? Never.
In our own self-pity, do we ever gain the understanding of others? Never.

No matter what your circumstances, you can't afford self-pity. It will only serve to make you miserable.

> *Give self-pity an inch and it will take a mile.*

If you want to be:
>   Filled with gloom,
>   Taken over by sadness,
>   Without friends,
>   Physically ill,
>   Problem-beaten,

Then go ahead—feel sorry for yourself! But if you want the good life—slam the door on self-pity.

To get rid of self-pity, do these six things:

1. *Spot it quickly and see it for what it is.* Sooner or later selfishness brings us to a state of mind of self-pity. What else is self-pity except simply centering on one's miserable self; seeing everything that's wrong, nothing that is right. There is no getting around it, self-pity is pure selfishness.

2. *Exercise your power to choose something better than self-pity.* The story is told about a young football star who had lost his mother just a couple of days before the big game. The coach didn't know what to do; this was his very best player. He did not have a suitable replacement for his star at quarterback. It was the big game to decide the championship. But the coach felt like he should leave the decision concerning playing up to the boy. No one expected the young man to show up for the game. The night of the big game came. The teams ran out on the field—the young star with them. While the team went through their pre-game warm-ups, the young football star went over to the stands. A couple of rows up in the stands there was an empty seat; it was draped in black. The young boy stood there and looked at the empty seat and said, "Mother, I'm playing this game for you." Then he went out on the field and played better than he had ever played before, and led his team to victory.

This splendid story illustrates so well that no matter what happens, you still choose how you're going to react. This young man could have sat down and started to cry, he could have felt sorry for himself, made himself the object of sympathy of all his fellow teammates. He could have made them all so sorry that the entire team would have been affected and the game would have been lost. Yes, he hurt, as we hurt when bad things happen to us, but he refused to mix that hurt with the defeating ingredient of self-pity. Do it—bar the door against private enemy number one—self-pity.

Choose to make self-pity the unwelcome guest in your mind.

*Exercise your God-given power of choice.*

3. *Make use of physical exercise.* There is tremendous value in physical exercise. Going through the trauma of divorce, I was in a mental stew. Trying to figure this out and that out, my mind was so tired from analyzing that I found myself bogged down in the state of mental confusion. A wise friend wanted to help, so he bought me a membership in a health club close to my work. Then he came by and picked me up three mornings a week, and accompanied me down to the gym to work out with vigorous exercise. First, this helped me to get my mind off myself and my problems. Second, as my body began to shape up and tone up, it helped to rebuild my self-image. Third, with the discipline and control over my physical body came the needed strength to control my mind and kick self-pity out the door. In addition, this exercise made my body tired so I could sleep at night, even though I was torn up emotionally.

4. *Expect some heartache along the way.* Jesus warned in John 16:33, "In the world ye shall have tribulation." He never even suggested that there was the slightest possibility that one could pass through life without feeling the sting of disappointment, or experiencing the sharp knife of emotional hurt. This world is our preparation, our proving ground for a better world. Remember:

It is the struggles that make a man strong.

It is the hardships that make a man an overcomer.

It is the obstacles that provide a man his greatest opportunities.

Particularly bothered by the unjust and unfair criticisms that I felt, I talked to my preacher father by phone. After I had poured out all the various ways in which I was being mistreated, my dad said, "Son, you're just going to have to get tough-skinned." At the time I didn't like that very much. As I thought about it in the days ahead, I found out what tremendous advice this was—not to be so easily hurt, not to put too much concern in what others think.

*It is far more important to please God than man.*

5. *Focus all your attention on what you have, not on what you have lost.* So many people are beaten because they center on their

lack, loss, limitations. Think on these three, and you'll feel sorry for yourself every time. That was one of my big problems. I had been thinking about all I had lost. I'd lost my wife, my two children; I'd lost the respect of a lot of people, and was about to lose the church I pastored. I had lost my place and position in the denomination. About this time I went to see a friend who had a saying hanging on the wall above his desk so that any person coming into his office complaining could read it. Here is what it said: "I complained because I had no shoes, till I met a man who had no feet."

Right then and there I began to take inventory on what I had. I still had my health, thank the Lord for that. I had ten years of experience and know-how as a pastor; if I needed to, I could start over. Besides, I had the valuable lessons that God was daily teaching me through this tragedy. I had two wonderful parents who believed in me and were standing by me with their support and prayers. I had some friends who were pulling for me during this time. Most of all, I had God, who was bigger than anything that was wrong in my life.

On the most tragic day of history an innocent man fell into a strange, unfair set of circumstances. Simon, a visitor to Jerusalem from North Africa, was in the crowd watching as they took Jesus out to crucify him. Before he could get away, the soldiers forced him to carry the load of the cross Jesus had fallen under. There was not one thing Simon could do to escape. He was the victim of cruel circumstances.

What happened to Simon of Cyrene happens to us. A set of circumstances is forced upon us and we are caught. We are compelled to live with the difficult. Sometimes it is an illness in the family, a financial burden, or a heavy responsibility. Whatever, it seems unfair and we feel like a victim of circumstances. What appeared to be a cruel set of circumstances, turned out to be the greatest thing that ever happened to Simon. Because of this, he came to know Jesus. He discovered that in Christ he was not a victim of circumstances, but a victor over circumstances.

> *Victor over circumstances instead of victim of circumstances. With God's help—that's you!*

"In all these things we are more than conquerors through him that loved us" (Romans 8:37). It is God's plan for you to be the victor over circumstances, not the victim of circumstances. Accept this truth: "And we know that all things work together for good to them that love God" (Romans 8:28). And believe that, no matter what, you will be a victor.

It's not what you have *lost,* it's what you *have* that counts. It's not what seems impossible, it is the fact that with God, all things are possible. That makes the difference. Don't worry about what you can't do, but look at what you can do now.

Stand up to life—and move ahead.

So you failed—so what?

So you aren't as beautiful as so and so—so what?

So your life is tough—so what?

So your daughter has gone wrong—so what?

So your mate has left you—so what?

So you dad was a drunk—so what?

So you're deserving of a better job—so what?

Big question—what are you going to do about it—feel sorry for yourself? Never!

*With God's help, make the best out of the worst.*

With God's help, you, too, can turn your disappointments into an appointment to beat the bad with something good, to make up the loss with greater gain.

*Whatever is wrong, is my opportunity, with God's help, to make it right.*

6. *Give yourself in service to others.* There are always a lot of other people you can feel sorry for instead of yourself. Since self-pity is a direct result of self-centeredness, there is no better cure for selfishness than giving oneself to others.

My sure cure for self-pity in my life is to just go visiting in the homes of people in our parish. As I give myself to other people, it's not long until I've forgotten about myself. There is great joy in giving yourself to others.

Paul and Silas were in jail in Philippi. It was a cruel experience for them. Finally, when they were released from being imprisoned in the smelly dungeon, they went to the house of Lydia to visit with the other Christians. Now if this had been you or me, we probably would have said, "Get me to bed quickly," "Get me something to eat," "Send for a doctor," or "I had a terrible time." And we would get everyone to feel sorry for us because we had been in prison for the Lord's work. Not Paul and Silas, though. They didn't even sit down and allow the others to comfort them. Instead, they chose to comfort the others. They had no time for self-pity, they ceased not "to teach and preach Jesus Christ." Give yourself in service to others and you won't even have time to think about self-pity.

> *Thank you, Jesus, because your way of giving one-self to others is the happy, healthy way to live.*

# 5

# Apply Healing Medicine to Your Emotional Wounds

The total physical pain I have experienced in my life doesn't even begin to compare with the emotional pain that I suffered during the trauma of going through my divorce. Nothing hurts more in this world than to be wounded in your spirit.

When God made us, what a marvelous combination he put within us in giving us the capacity to think and feel. This gives us the potential for ecstasy on one hand and agony on the other. Being made as we are, and our world being what it is, there is no person alive who will pass through life without suffering some emotional pain. To go a step further, I seriously doubt there is anyone who lives who can escape being unjustly treated at some time by another person. This mistreatment of one another is the direct result of man's broken relationship with God.

No one has ever suffered emotional insult and injury more than Jesus. He was rejected, lied against, turned against by people he counted on, betrayed by close friends, unable to get even his mother to understand why he must die. He was called blasphemer, ridiculed, laughed at, and scorned. The physical suffering which was inflicted upon Jesus did not compare with the emotional pain he bore. Never once did Jesus react in word or deed to strike back and bring injury to those who were hurting him. Such inner strength! Always a responder instead of a reactor. No one has ever lived like Jesus. Jesus—our perfect example of how to overcome evil with good.

*Jesus was hurt that we might be healed.*

*What happens to you isn't nearly as important as how you react to what happens.*

When you get hurt, will you choose to react or respond? You're the only one who can decide the answer—but your answer will determine whether or not you will be:

Free or enslaved.

Responding or reacting.

Expanding or withdrawing.

Victor or victim.

Like Christ or like this world.

Fantastic insight! No one else causes our feelings—we cause our own feelings by our choice of responses and emotional re-actions. Someone may insult you, but it does not become your problem until you let it get under your skin. No one can make you angry unless you let him. When another person does something to you that hurts you, it cannot keep on hurting you unless you let it.

*If you go on hurting emotionally long after the injury, you have no one to blame but yourself.*

It is of utmost importance how we handle hurt. This is why Jesus told us: "The law of Moses says, 'If a man gouges out another's eye, he must pay with his own eye. If a tooth gets knocked out, knock out the tooth of the one who did it.' But I say: Don't resist violence. If you are slapped on one cheek, turn the other too" (Matthew 5:38, 39, TLB).

*Don't bury your hurts.* Years ago I worked with a woman who appeared to have a very fine Christian marriage. Apparently, there was little or no quarreling or conflict in her home. Actually this dear lady was repressing unsolved problems and hurts inside her. She thought they were forgotten, until suddenly one day they surfaced from her unconscious mind into her conscious mind and exploded. The emotional storm was uncontrollable! The hate and bitterness poured out like an erupting volcano. It caused her to do things in a pattern of hurt reactions that she would never have dreamed possible only months before.

One man shared this: "My wife and I often repressed our small annoyances with each other as unimportant and unworthy of notice. We said nothing about them and tried to forget them, which meant letting them slip unsolved into the reservoir of the unconscious. Then some trivial remark or incident would arise later and would trigger all the repressed feelings, which would rush to the surface as one. The result: An argument, or perhaps a quarrel was out of all proportion to the incident that caused it. The answer we found for this was never to bury our hurts but to be honest about them and speak of them at the time they occurred.''

*Don't withdraw.* Naturally none of us wants to be hurt. When hurt, the first impulse is to pull back into a shell so we cannot be hurt again. It is true that when we love, we leave ourselves open to be hurt. But without love, we are going to hurt so much more. It is people who do not receive love and who do not give love who continue to live in a hurting state. If you are hurt in love, the best thing you can do is love again. Because it's loving again that brings healing.

A joke is told about a young man who was dancing with his best girlfriend while another boy kept breaking in. Finally, he stopped, took off his glasses and said to his girl, ''Will you please hold my glasses?'' The girl became anxious and said, ''Oh, you aren't going to fight him are you?'' ''No, I just can't stand the sight of him.'' We must not withdraw from people. Isolation will only cause whatever hurt is within us to fester and hurt all the more.

*Don't retreat from something good just because you have been hurt.* A man in his forties became concerned because he found it difficult to care deeply for other people. Although he loved his wife and daughter he was unable to show much affection to them. As he was asking God to help him become a warm person, it all came back to him. As a young teenager, he had been rejected by a girl he cared for and had vowed, ''Never again will I be hurt like this. Never will I care enough for anyone to let them hurt me.'' Now, I ask you, who was the loser all these many years? To withdraw is to leave the game—sit on the sidelines while life passes by. To withdraw is to go on hurting—hurting—hurting—all alone.

Don't you do it. Do not allow any emotional hurt to take you out of the mainstream of life. Don't ever say:

I'll never trust anyone again.

I've been hurt once and never again.

I'll never try it in business another time.

I'll never believe in God again.

I'll never love again.

Don't allow anything that has happened to you to put you off the game.

*Don't take on someone else's hurts.* Joan had a problem—I was her problem. And yet to my knowledge I had done nothing to her personally, or said anything that should cause her to feel badly toward me, let alone hate me. The hatred was in her eyes. Joan had been a very smiling, jolly person around the church. But she now came to church with a very sour look on her face, with her lips actually turned downward, and as I preached, she glared at me with hatred. My heart went out to her because I knew that she had taken on herself the hurts of my divorcing wife, and it was eating her up. If I had done something to hurt her, I could go to her and say, "I'm wrong, I'm sorry I've hurt you, would you please forgive me?" Then the relationship could be healed. But under the circumstances, there was nothing I could do but wait, and pray that she might be healed of her ill feelings.

How glad I was when Joan asked me if she could come to my office for a talk. After she was seated, she started pouring out all the ill feelings she had for me. When it was my turn I said, "Joan, I am sorry if I have done anything to hurt you. Would you please tell me what it is I have done so I can ask you to forgive me." Then the truth hit her. I had not done anything to her at all, but she had borrowed hurt from another hurt person. These borrowed hurts were actually making her sick physically. The hatred she had toward me was occupying most of her time, dissipating most of her energy.

It was a great moment of personal growth for Joan when she saw the folly of borrowing someone else's hurt. It was a glorious day as our relationship was mended, because the minute Joan stopped borrowing the hurt, she was healed. To be another person's friend when they are hurting does not mean that you are to become your own enemy by borrowing their hurt.

*Don't hold on to your hurts*—the truth is, the more you hold on to hurts, the longer and more intense will your hurt become. As I try to help people, I sometimes get the feeling their emotional hurts are their cherished friends. At least they cling to their hurts like they just couldn't get along without them. To cling to your hurts like they were your last few cents doesn't make good sense. So let go of it—it's no good for you.

A wounded spirit becomes the target for these diseases. Hate —resentment—bitterness. These diseases produce ill feelings. Hate, resentment, bitterness infect an emotional wound in a way that prevents healing. When you're hurting emotionally, you can expect one or more or all these diseases to attack where you are wounded. For your own good, keep them out. If they do get into your wound, the next best thing you can do is to eliminate them as quickly as possible. The worst thing you can do is to let these germs remain in your open wound.

*To be healed, eliminate these emotional diseases: resentment–hate–bitterness.*

Attack the deadly disease of resentment—one of the most damaging germs you can get in your mind is that of resentment. So many people fail to understand the terrible price they pay for harboring resentment. The broken friendship, the loss of efficiency, the demoralized home life, the development of psychosomatic illnesses, the loss of energy, the negative view of life itself. All of these are part of what happens when this disease of resentment grips one's mind.

*Resentment is poison in the human mind and heart.* It poisons the relationship between man and man, woman and woman, husband and wife. I have witnessed resentment poison the entire atmosphere of a church. It does not take many people filled with resentment to create an atmosphere in a group that is anything but joyful and filled with love.

*Resentment drives people apart. It never brings them together.*

You have to keep a sharp lookout for the disease of resentment. Because it is very difficult to recognize resentment in oneself, we become very skillful in justifying ourselves. He or she did that, so it is all right if I do this. It is always the other guy who showed the ill will, said the spiteful words, did hateful things. What the other guy did, doesn't hurt us nearly as deeply as our own resentment. Resentment is infection in an open wound.

*Unresolved resentment is far more damaging to the person who harbors it than it is to the object of it.*

I'm sure there are times when our grieved spirit is fully justifiable, but, justified or not, no one can hold on to resentment without hurting himself many times more than he is already hurt. Resentment multiplies the original hurt one hundred times.

I heard about a man whose young, attractive wife was killed by a drunken motorist. This man was left to face the world alone with twin children—a boy and a girl. To be broken in sorrow for a while is understandable, but when the shock had passed, and the edge had come off his grief, he burned with a concentrated hate against his wife's "murderer." Always (and not without justification) he referred to the drunken motorist as the "murderer."

As a result of his resentments, his home became a bad place in which to live. His children felt they had not only lost a mother to death, but a father to hate. All the while the children suffered while this man maintained his hate out of some twisted loyalty to his wife's memory. On this grounds he justified his bitter spirit. There was no cure until that beautiful day when he sought God's help, asked God for forgiveness, and asked God to heal his deep sorrow.

*Pour out the poison of resentment so your wounds can heal.*

*Unchecked resentment turns to hate.* There is no more destructive disease of mind or body than hate. Believe it or not, hate is far more destructive to the mind than cancer is to the body.

Hate can make you do irrational things. Last April, my older brother told me about a fine restaurant in a large American city, where he liked to go when on business there. The owner was obviously making piles of money. Out of the blue, the owner sold his very successful business at a large loss. Why? As the news about town had it, the restaurant was being patronized by people of the Jewish race. And this owner hated Jews with a passion. So intense, so overpowering was his hatred, he sold out his business at a loss in order to get away from Jews. You say, How stupid. Yes, hate can make you do stupid things.

Hate can make you a murderer. You respond, "How ridiculous, I couldn't kill him." The Bible says, "Whosoever hateth his brother is a murderer: and ye know no murderer hath eternal life" (1 John 3:15). Hate is a desire to hurt, or make another pay. Some common ways it expresses itself are: Criticism, name-calling, snubbing, getting even. Ask God to root all hate out of you. Act now—do away with hate before it does away with you!

*God's answer to hate is to put love in its place.*

*Mix hate with your hurt and seek revenge and you become worse than the person you feel has done you wrong.*

In the story *Ben Hur,* the central character, Juda Ben Hur, returns to Israel intent on one thing—revenge. Because of one man, he has seen the sweet years of young manhood wasted down in the galley of a slave ship. His historic position and fortune has been desolated. Because of one man, his mother and sister are dying, rotting away as lepers in the cave outside Jerusalem. And now he lives for one thing, to avenge himself upon this man, to bring revenge upon Messala. The passion consumes Ben Hur to such an extent that his sweetheart, Esther, looking into his tortured eyes exclaims, "Juda Ben Hur, you have become a Messala."

*When you hate another person you become that person's slave.*

Hate enslaves one to the person he hates. Wherever he goes, the person he hates goes. His thoughts are dominated by the hated person. The way to be free is not to wipe the other person out, but to wipe out your hate.

On the historic date August 9, 1974, President Nixon, the first president in the history of America to be brought down to resignation, gave his personal farewell address to his staff, having just fallen from the highest position of power in the modern world. This is what Richard M. Nixon said: "Those who hate you don't win until you hate them back, and that will destroy you." Whether President Nixon deserved it or did not deserve it, he had just endured two years of deep emotional wounding. Richard Nixon has discovered that no matter how it hurts, no matter how wounded emotionally you are, one cannot afford to let the destructive disease of hatred infect his spirit. To do so is to destroy oneself.

> *Ask and God will do for you what you cannot do for yourself.*

*Dig bitterness out of the wound.* A couple of years after the divorce, I thought I had eliminated all the resentment, all the hatred, I was pretty well healed from my emotional wounds. Not only had I been hurt by the divorce itself, but was deeply hurt over becoming like a stranger in the church family I had belonged to since birth.

At a dinner party with friends, we were all enjoying ourselves. In the course of the conversation, something was said about a project the church I had formerly belonged to was planning. Before I knew it, I had reacted with a strong statement against the denomination. My host was shocked and looked at me and said, "Dale, that sounds like you are bitter." I have to admit I was more than a little surprised at myself, because I really thought my attitudes were more positive toward the denomination. But all of a sudden, here came this bitter statement. I apologized and asked the host to forgive me.

Later that evening, after arriving home, I went to prayer with my Heavenly Father. I said, "Lord, I want to go to the very root of this bitterness. I know that I am hurt over the fact I appear to be a stranger in the church family I was brought up in. They are still good people and I love them, and I want you to cleanse all this bitterness out of my wounds so I can heal up completely." There, before God, I poured all the bitterness out. I continued, "Now, Lord, take it all away and I promise you from this day forward with your help, I will never say anything that is not positive about this great church again." Thank God, that night all the bitterness was completely dug out. If you have any bitterness, let God dig it all out.

> *The sooner you apply healing to your hurt, the better. Delay only leaves the wounds wide open for infectious diseases.*

To heal a wounded spirit, take these seven steps:

*1. Tend to your attitudes and actions and stop worrying about what someone else has done or not done to you. Tell yourself it's useless to be all bent out of shape over what another person does or does not do. It is useless because:*

a. I cannot change another person, I can only change myself.
b. I'm not responsible to God for what he or she does; in other words, leave the judging to God.
c. The Bible tells us, "Vengeance is mine; I will repay, saith the Lord" Romans 12:19).

*No one can hurt you any more than you let them.*

### 2. Clean out the wound.

I shared with a middle-aged lady my experiences with hurt, and how I had cleaned out all the wounds and God had healed me so beautifully. Her face suddenly lit up and she said, "Yes, that is it." Then she began to talk of her childhood, especially about her mother who was dominating and never outwardly affectionate. She never felt her mother loved her, and it hurt. As a child, she never seemed able to win any approval. Everything she did was wrong!

As we talked, a new revelation came to this lady. She saw that the whole pattern of her life had been set by her unhealed childhood hurts. For years she had cherished these hurts and felt sorry for herself. Firmly she had held on to the picture of being an unloved child and in so doing, had filled her life with resentment. Everywhere she had gone, her ill feeling went along. She said, "I see it at last, and now it is all finished."

From past experience, I knew that this was not true. She would not be free from this hurt and its accompanying resentment until she gave it to God to resolve. So I asked her to give it all to God, aloud, in detail. Sometimes our pride tries to hinder us from making a definite, specific transaction such as this. This was true in her case. Her first prayer was vague and she was quite unaware she had given nothing. I explained this to her and asked her to give up the hurt and the resentment. This time she gave the hurt and the feeling of guilt about the resentment, but not the resentment itself.

Again I told her she had not really given up her resentment. She became very annoyed with me until she saw it was true. She had not put her prayer in words that were specific and final.

This time she laughed and said, "God, you must think I'm stupid. I do give you my resentment." A week later I had a letter from which I quote: "There is such a singing and freedom inside me because of the discovery we made. I did not realize how bad that was and what a release it is to be free from those hidden resentments. My husband thinks he has a new wife; my mother has a new daughter. I am a new person!"

> *A big step to your emotional healing is to open up, to open up to God.*

### 3. Practice forgiveness.

There is nothing more healing in all the world than when one starts to practice forgiveness. It's not always easy to forgive, but it's far more difficult not to. When Jesus was so unjustly treated, how did he react? The answer is he didn't react, he responded. Jesus —the responder—forgave them. Jesus cried as the blood spurted from his heart, "Father, forgive them, for they know not what they do." Jesus taught that we were to forgive an unlimited number of times (Matthew 18:21, 22). Disciples asked the Lord how many times they should forgive and Jesus said seven times seventy. Then he added that if we don't forgive others, then we can't be forgiven our sins.

> *Only the offended can forgive.*[1]

A wife was left alone evening after evening. Her resentments turned to hate. She started keeping a hate book, actually writing down in a notebook every night her husband was gone from home, and the exact number of minutes. It got so bad he spent only two evenings home in seven weeks, always finding excuses to be away. His wife would constantly badger him about this in the few minutes he would be home.

Then the lady began to respond to God's working in her heart. He showed her what her bitter unforgiving spirit was doing, how in the few minutes her husband was at home, she was driving him further and further away from home and herself. She read the challenge of Christ in her Bible, to be the first to forgive. Her life took a turn for the better when she said with God's help, "I forgive him." Then she had a second great thought. If she was going to forgive him, it meant throwing the hate book away. She took the hate book and threw it in the fire. That was followed by a great idea. The idea was this—"I will make the most out of those

[1]Robert Schuller, *Self Love: The Dynamic Force of Success* (New York: Hawthorn Books, Inc., 1969), p. 100.

moments when he is home, and make it interesting and pleasant

Within weeks he began spending more time at home and soon afterward he faced up to the way he had been shortchanging his family. Foundations were laid for a new and more satisfying relationship in the home. Forgiveness is what brought the breath of fresh air and newness to this home.

*Forgiveness has healed many a broken relationship,*
*and forgiveness has healed many a wounded spirit.*

The healing medicine—forgiveness—is yours for the using.

*4. Pray for those who despitefully use you.*

A man said to me, "How can I get rid of my deep resentment toward the man who has caused me to lose my job?" Here is what I said: "Pray for him." He almost fell off his chair. He said, "Do what?" "Pray for him. Jesus said to pray for your enemies." He said: "You have got to be kidding." I said, "Try it, it will work wonders for your attitude." Nothing neutralizes resentment like prayer.

I continued, "Believe me, I know it is a difficult thing to do. The last several months I have found myself the target of quite a bit of criticism from Christian people I have known for a long time. Christ's way is not always the easy way, but it is certainly the best way. As I prayed for these people who had hurt me, the hurt I felt was healed and in place of having ill feelings toward these people, there is love and understanding of why they feel the way they do. Try it in your life and see if it doesn't make all the difference." He promised me he would.

A couple of weeks later, I saw my friend following the Sunday morning service. I asked him how he was coming along in praying for his enemy. He said, "Pastor, it really works! I am even beginning to understand why the guy did it. God has given me a love for him." Happy tears rolled down my friend's cheeks. Nothing answers the problem of resentment like prayer.

*Pray for those who mistreat you–and you will be*
*free from all ill feelings!*

*5. Make allowances for those who hurt you.*

Jesus said, "They know not what they do." The ability of seeing good in others in spite of what they do is an added antidote against having resentment and hate. Go ahead—give others the benefit of the doubt—you have everything to gain and nothing to lose.

> *Blessed are the peacemakers: for they shall be call-*
> *ed the children of God (Matthew 5:9).*

6. *Let God heal your broken spirit.*

> *God is at my elbow and yours.*

There is nothing that makes you sick, but what Jesus can heal —Jesus the Great Physician.

> You may feel that there's no hope,
> Broken hearts just cannot mend.
> Though you're torn in many pieces,
> God can make you whole again.
> Storms of doubt go all directions,
> But don't you be afraid.
> God can make all corrections,
> He made a body out of clay.
> Pick up the broken pieces
> And bring them to the Lord.
> Pick up the broken pieces
> Trust in His Holy Word.
> He will put them back together
> And make your life complete.
> Just place the broken pieces
> At the Savior's feet.[2]

When I was in my senior year at Olivet College in Illinois, I was a custodian of the large college church. One Saturday as I was cleaning the sanctuary, I had the windows open and a little bird flew in. Once inside, the bird flew around, having a big time, looking that huge church over. What an adventure, so exciting and new. And then all of a sudden, it dawned on the little bird he was trapped inside the sanctuary; at least it seemed that way to me as I watched him. Then he began to fly back through the air looking for some way out of the church building. I found myself wanting to help the trapped panic-stricken bird. After awhile, he landed upstairs in the balcony. I ran up the stairs. You would have thought I was crazy if you had been watching me. As I reached

[2]From "Broken Pieces" by James Martin, Jr. and Ruby Kitchen, © 1968 by John T. Benson, Jr. Used by permission.

down to pick up the little bird, he took off again. Back downstairs I went, from one end of the church to the other, following him. Up against the top of the window it hit, trying to escape its captivity, but could not find its way out. The struggle went on for a long time.

Then in utter exhaustion, giving up, the bird fell to the floor. He was not dead, but he must have felt half-dead. I walked over to where he was, knelt down, reached out my hands, and gently picked up the fallen bird. I carried the bird in my hand over to the window and opened my hands, and the little bird flapped his wings and flew away—with new life. He was free—free to fly and climb the heights again.

Just a few years ago I was broken, torn apart emotionally, trying this way and that to find a solution. Then one day, completely exhausted, not knowing what to do or how to get out of my situation, I fell into the loving hands of my Heavenly Father. He picked me up. He nursed my wounds with his love. He held me close to his heart. He healed me of all my brokenness and made me whole. God has set me free to fly to the heights again. You, too, can have your wounded spirit completely healed.

*God specializes in making the broken whole.*

### 7. Overcome evil by doing good.

It's not God's plan for you to be run over by evil or overpowered by things that happen to you. With his help, take the initiative. Initiate good actions toward those who have wronged you. Live the positive good life that Christ called you to live, no matter what anyone else does, and before you know it, you will be healthy, happy and completely whole inside.

Someone asked me the question, Where would you be without your wounds? I thank God I was cut to the core emotionally, because out of that has come my greatest personal growth. Tragedy has made me a more useful minister for God. I am now far more understanding and compassionate with hurting people. I often spot the hurt in their eyes before they even open their mouths. I have an unshakable faith in a God who can heal all hurt and make the wounded whole. Out of my brokenness God has brought the very best to my life. You, too, can be completely healed of all your hurts! If you are broken, you too can be made whole!

# 6

# Choose and Cultivate a Positive Attitude

A man with a positive attitude may be knocked down, but never beaten. Many will say there is no way, but a man with a positive attitude will always find a way. Multitudes of people never achieve because they give up. The positive man is a high achiever because he never gives up. The positive person, whether he knows our Achiever's Creed or not, lives by it. Based on Philippians 4:13, here it is:

> Whatever the mind can conceive
> and I will dare to believe,
> with God's help, I can achieve.

Next to knowing Jesus Christ personally as Lord and Savior, there is nothing more important than having a positive mental attitude. Your attitude can:

> Make you or break you.
> Heal you or hurt you.
> Make you friends or make you enemies.
> Put you uptight or put you at ease.
> Make you miserable or make you happy.
> Make you a failure or make you an achiever.

Some people today think the whole world stinks. Once a cranky grandpa lay down to take a nap. To have a little fun, his grandson put some limburger cheese on his mustache under his nose. Grandpa awoke with a snort, charged out of the bedroom and shouted, "This room stinks!" On through the house he went, shouting louder, "This whole house stinks!" He charged out on the porch and shouted as loud as he could, "The whole world stinks!" The truth is, it was Grandpa who stunk. The problem was under his own nose. Ninety-nine times out of 100, when we begin to feel like things stink, the problem is not with the world or with others, but ourselves. Our own attitudes have become negative. Change negative attitudes to positive ones, and you change your world.[1]

*To live in a better world, become a positive thinker.*

Henry J. Kaiser tells this personal story about one time when he was building a levee along a river bank. There came a great storm and flood which buried all of his earth-moving machinery and destroyed the work that had been done. Upon going out to observe the damage after the water receded, he found his workers standing around glumly looking at the mud and the buried machinery.

He came among them and said with a smile, "Why are you so glum?"

"Don't you see what has happened?" they asked. "Our machinery is covered with mud."

"What mud?" he asked brightly.

"What mud!" they repeated in astonishment. "Look around you. It is a sea of mud."

"Oh," he laughed, "I don't see any mud."

"But how can you say that?" they asked him.

"Because," said Mr. Kaiser, "I am looking at a clear blue sky, and there is no mud up there. There is only sunshine, and I never saw any mud that could stand against sunshine. Soon it will be dried up, and then you will be able to move your machinery and start all over again." What makes the difference between seeing mud and seeing sunshine? The difference is in attitude.

> *In the final analysis, it is your own attitude that will make you or break you, not what has happened to you.*

[1]From *Life is Tremendous,* Charlie, "Tremendous" Jones, Tyndale House Publishers, 1968, p. 14. Used by permission.

## THE POWER TO CHOOSE YOUR ATTITUDE IS YOURS.

Without a doubt, the human mind is the most awe-inspiring creation of God. The mind of man would stand above all the other miracles of Creation if they were listed in an order of importance. What you can do with your mind is really fantastic. Within it you have a will, the ability to reason, the feelings of emotions, the ability to reach beyond with your imagination, the inner conscience, the five physical senses, the recorder of memory, the sixth sense, and the subconscious. When one thinks about the human mind that the Master Creator has created for us, he has to stand in utter amazement.

### Exercise mind control.

Who controls your mind? You do! Your mind is the one thing over which the Creator has given you complete control. God, himself, will not set this aside or reverse it, or do anything to change it. To you, God has given the right and the ability to control your own mind.

In the midst of my divorce when each day was a fight for survival, I came across the story of Dr. Victor Frankl. As this courageous man stood under the glaring lights of the Gestapo court in a Nazi concentration camp, soldiers took from him every earthly possession—his clothes, watch, even his wedding ring. Dr. Frankl said that as he stood there naked, his body shaved, he was destitute but for one thing. It was something that no one could take away from him. He realized in that moment that he still had the power to choose his own attitude. In my broken situation a lot of things were out of my control. For a controlled person like myself, this was most difficult. But the one thing I still had was the power to choose my own attitudes.

### No matter what happens the attitude choice is still yours.

I am not responsible for anyone's attitudes and actions but my own. What an important principle this is! Especially is this important for all those who are now hurting from what they feel someone else has done or is doing. Hundreds of times in my journey from brokenness to wholeness I had to remind myself of this truth: I am responsible for no one else's attitudes and actions, but I am responsible to God for my own attitudes and actions. I discovered that when my own attitudes and actions were right, I could live with myself and enjoy good feelings toward others.

No shattering experience leaves one where it found him. It is the attitude that determines where the emotional heartbreak will leave him. By the choice of your own attitude, your heartbreak can remain with you or you can leave it behind. "Life," someone said, "is 10 percent what happens to you, and 90 percent how you react to what happens to you." No matter what happens to you, choose positive thoughts and sooner or later, you will be the winner. On the other hand, if you give in to negative thoughts, allowing them to dwell within your mind, there is no way that you will be anything but the loser.

Your attitude is far more important than anything else.

Your attitude is more important than:

Facts

Circumstances

What others say

Your past

Your education

Money

Dr. Samuel Shoemaker tells the delightful story of an elderly woman who was knocked down by a tire that flew off a passing truck. The accident left her with a broken hip and confined her to a small room for the rest of her days. There is always the chance that one will grow bitter, or at least become impatient with such circumstances. Not that lovely lady! When Dr. Shoemaker stood by her in the hospital, she looked up from her bed of intense pain and, with a wonderful smile, said, "Well, I wonder what God has for me to do here." What a beautiful, positive attitude.

When trouble bowls you over, when you are at the bottom emotionally, it's still a matter of choice. No one else can decide for you. You alone must choose whether you'll let trouble lick you, or whether you'll take courage and, with God's help, lick the trouble. There is nothing in this world that can happen to you but what, with God's help, and with a positive attitude, you can come out on top.

*Created to be the master over circumstances, not to be mastered by them—that's you!*

My close friend Tom Burton is mastering some very difficult circumstances with a persistent positive attitude. Two years ago Tom owned three survey companies in the State of Oregon, and one construction company. At that time he had more than one hundred people working for him. However, through a chain of reverses, Tom found himself having more in liabilities against his companies than he had assets. For two years he went through the grueling, painful process of winding all the businesses down, trying to satisfy all the creditors when there wasn't enough money to even begin to go around. He was being harassed and hammered by multitudes of people demanding payment, and for the first time did not know where the next paycheck was going to come from to provide for his family. Talk about going through deep, troubled waters! He and his family have been through it.

During those many months I never heard my friend even once say any word to even imply that he was beaten. Instead, I heard him say, "We'll make it, we'll put the past behind us." "I'll get it going again." "When I build it the next time, it will be better, and I won't make all the mistakes I made in the past." Tom is making it, and he's going to make it bigger and better than it ever was before. I can predict this because Tom has two of life's most worthwhile ingredients:

1. He has the wisdom to learn from all his experiences.

2. He has a positive attitude that will not quit. Tom believes that, with Christ's help, he can do anything. With Christ's help you, too, can overcome.

*Attitude is more important than fact.*

## TWELVE WAYS YOU CAN ELIMINATE THE NEGATIVE AND ACTIVATE THE POSITIVE

To get out of the slump, to get over the hurdle, to get up and get going again, you've got to do something. A positive attitude isn't something that will just come to you automatically. Neither will it come to you by just living defensively. You must go on the offensive—do something—act! Here is what you can do to become that more positive person that you want to be.

1. *Become an ambassador of good words to every person you meet every day.* During the gas crisis in the winter of 1974, I drove into our neighborhood service station. At that time around the gas stations, everyone's nerves were on edge because of long lines and not being able to buy gas when they wanted it. Many of the attendants became the object of the public's frustrations. Having waited a long time in line, I finally got up to the gas pump. The young man there gave me a big smile and said, "Hello, how are you today?" In spite of some trying circumstances, he had determined to spread good cheer and friendliness to everyone. He really gave me a lift. Now each time I go back to that station, and he is there, I am especially friendly and cheerful to him. Jesus taught that if we give, we will receive. That attendant gave to me, and he has received back many cheerful hellos. To fill your life with joy, give cheerful words to everyone you meet.

2. *No matter what happens, look for the good and you'll find it.* A positive thinker does not refuse to recognize the negative, he refuses to dwell on it. Positive thinking is a form of thought which habitually looks for the best results from the worst conditions. It is always possible to look for something good; to expect the best for yourself even though things look bad. And the remarkable fact is that when you seek good, you will find it.

This past spring my friend Pat Fettig walked through the "valley of the shadow of death." His twenty-four-year-old brother, Freddie, drowned in the Sandy River on a Sunday afternoon. For three long days Pat and others searched up and down the rugged rapids of the Sandy River looking for the body. A chain of prayer was put into action at New Hope on Wednesday. Thursday morning I was there when the divers pulled the body out. As we were riding back to town, after having been through the ordeal of a lifetime, he looked at me and with a big, positive smile, he said, "Praise God, we found him. Thank you, Jesus!" Refuse to dwell on the negative. In every happening, look for the good.

Mary was an attractive woman in her early thirties who had been active in her church. She came to see me in my office to tell me she had had it with her husband. This very day she was going to see a lawyer and file for divorce against Frank. Surprised, I invited her to sit down and tell me about it. For the next hour I listened to a story about a monster, her husband. By the time she got finished I, too, thought it was all over. I felt sorry for the poor lady putting up with all this mistreatment. To myself, I thought, "Frank doesn't deserve a fine woman like Mary for his wife." However, my better judgment prevailed and I handed Mary a paper on which to draw. "Mary," I said, "I want you to draw a circle. Now put one black dot in there for everything that is wrong with your husband, Frank." I could tell she was really enjoying putting the dots in the circle. When she finally could not think of anything else, I said, "Mary, tell me what you see in that circle."

"Oh, a bunch of dirty old dots," she said.

"Mary, tell me what else you see."

"Just black dots, lots of them," she answered.

"Mary, how much of the total space in the circle is taken up by the dots? I want you to look at that other space, lots and lots of it, in comparison to the space taken up by the dots. Mary, before you go to see the lawyer, tell me about all the other, I mean all of Frank's good points."

At first it was hard for her to get started. But it got easier and easier as she shared Frank's good points. A miracle happened; her whole attitude changed, and to this day she is still married to Frank. Take the bigger look and see all the good.

3. *By an act of your will, fill your mind with what is positive.* The Bible tells us how to do it. Philippians 4:8—"Fix your thoughts on what is true and good and right. Think about things that are pure and lovely, and dwell on the fine, good things in others. Think about all you can praise God for and be glad about" (TLB).

One of the greatest builders of positive attitudes given in the Bible is also one of the hardest to swallow. Here it is: "In every thing give thanks: for this is the will of God in Christ Jesus concerning you" (1 Thessalonians 5:18).

When are we to give thanks?

In suffering? Yes.

When treated unfairly? Yes.

When misunderstood? Yes.

When taken advantage of? Yes.

When things go well? Yes.

When things go wrong? Yes.

*Give thanks in everything.*

The Apostle Paul knew what he wrote about when he said, "Giving thanks always for all things unto God" (Ephesians 5:20). The Apostle's mission to Philippi was a big failure. Instead of being followed by eager listeners, Paul and his co-workers were seized, beaten, and thrown into a musty jail, where their feet were made fast in the stocks. There, instead of whining and complaining and looking on the dark side, they sang and gave thanks to God. Their thanksgiving was no more dependent on outward circumstances than was that of Jesus when on the same night he was betrayed, he took bread and gave thanks.

I have witnessed the most exciting, miraculous things in people's lives when they have really practiced this principle of giving thanks in everything. Dare to give thanks in everything and you, too, will see miracles.

*All sunshine and no rain makes a desert.*

4. *Never surrender to negative emotions.* When you feel the mighty onrush of a negative emotion, how do you handle it? Admit it, face it, but don't give in to it. A sure way to fight weeds is to plant thick, healthy grass. The way to destroy a negative emotion is to verbalize a positive statement. You counterattack the invading negative emotion by shooting the positive counterpart. How? By using an affirmation that will release the positive emotion. For instance, you feel bad because you can't quit smoking. You don't verbalize it negatively: "I wish I could quit smoking." By saying this you surrender to, and are overpowered by, this negative force. Instead say, "I enjoy not smoking." "I love the feeling of being free from an enslaving habit." "I love the clean taste in my mouth since I have stopped smoking." By uttering these positive words, you have started stopping.

5. *Practice the principle of replacement.* For every negative emotion there's a positive emotion that can be selected by you to eliminate the negative one. Replace:

Anger with love,
Fear with faith,
Despair with hope,
Greed with generosity,
Sorrow with joy,

Complaint with gratitude,
Worry with trust,
Guilt with forgiveness.

6. *Bar the suggestive, the lewd, the perverted, the immoral, and the vulgar from your mind.* You can't feed on garbage and stay healthy and sound in mind. The Bible warns us: "Don't let the world squeeze you into its mold" (Romans 12:2, Phillips). "Be ye transformed by the renewing of your mind" (Romans 12:2, KJV). How do we keep our minds healthy and clean? By living in fellowship with God—living God's way instead of the way of the world.

> *Put garbage into your mind—you're going to get garbage out. Put good thoughts into your mind—and good actions will come out.*

7. *See good in others.* We all know people who create a negative atmosphere wherever they go. Why? Because they like to talk about everything and everyone in a negative way. Watch this—see if it is not true. Every time you talk negatively about another human being, you infect the atmosphere with bad feelings.

Years ago I knew a pastor who had something good to say about everyone. This man, although not highly educated for his calling, was a tremendous success; everyone loved him. Who wouldn't love such a positive person? Look for the good in everybody you meet and you will find it.

8. *Determine to take an attitude of love and goodwill toward others.* There is nothing uglier than a bad attitude. Like the pollution from a paper mill on a windy day, it makes everything stink. On the other hand there is nothing more beautiful than a good attitude toward other people. A good attitude will win you friends and influence people. A long time after issues are forgotten, people will remember you for your attitude, be it good or bad.

Change your attitude toward other people and other people will change their attitude toward you. Your attitude toward the people who are around you is always bound to transmit and communicate itself. They say that a dog knows when you do not like him. Well, if a dog knows when you do not like him, will not a human being, who is far more aware, sense your true feelings?

Essentially, getting people to like you is merely the other side of liking them. One of the very popular men of our century was the late Will Rogers. One of the statements that he made immortal was this: "I never met a man I didn't like." That may have been a slight fib, but I am sure Will Rogers did not regard it as such. That is the way people who knew him tell us he felt about people, and in return, people everywhere loved Will Rogers. Love people and they will love you back.

9. *Express appreciation and warm feelings to others.* Ninety-nine percent of the time, when bad thoughts are holding good thoughts out of our minds, it is because they are selfish thoughts. A common need of us all is to get our minds off ourselves.

The way to get your mind off yourself is to give yourself away. You can do this by expressing gratitude or words of appreciation, or showing love for another person. One of the most healing therapies in the world is to give oneself in friendship and service to another person.

*It's a healthy thing to give yourself away.*

10. *Practice positive prayer.* Several weeks ago on a Monday morning, two different people within an hour shared with me how they found themselves in a real state of confusion over the weekend due to happenings in their lives. But when they really got alone with God and poured it all out to him, there came peace within and ability to think clearly.

*Nothing clears the mind like prayer.*

The Bible has a lot to teach about how we can pray and anticipate a good outcome. Mark 11:24 (TLB) says, "You can pray for *anything,* and *if you believe, you have it; it's yours.*" That is a tremendous offer! Just think. Whatever you ask and pray for, if you believe that you receive it, you shall have it. And Mark 11:23 (TLB) says, "All that's required is that you really believe and have no doubt."

To practice believing is of primary importance. It is the winning force in any and all achievements. When you expect the best, you release a magnetic force in your mind which by a law of attraction tends to bring the best to you. But if you expect the worst, you release from your mind the power of repulsion which tends to force the best from you. It is absolutely amazing how believing the best can happily set in motion the powerful forces that make the best happen.

As you pray, fill your mind with these verses:

"If God be for us, who can be against us?" (Romans 8:31).

"They that wait upon the Lord shall renew their strength" (Isaiah 40:31).

"According to your faith be it unto you" (Matthew 9:29).

"I can do all things through Christ which strengtheneth me" (Philippians 4:13).

11. *You can count on it. God is good, and he has a plan for your life.* He will not fail you; he will not let you down. He will bring good out of bad. When Peter Marshall died, a prophetic voice was silenced at the age of 46. Catherine Marshall wrote: "On that chilly, January morning, 1949, as I looked at my husband's face for the last time, then turned to leave the bare little hospital room, it seemed like whistling in the dark to believe that God could bring good out of such tragic loss." But because of it, Catherine Marshall has found a capacity to write in a way that has ministered to multitudes of people in their needs.

When I find my enthusiasm level dropping below the high energy standard I have set for myself, I can usually pinpoint the trouble—"I am not expecting anything much to happen today!" The solution is simple. Plan something big! Get an exciting idea and put it into action. It is so much fun to live expectantly.

12. *Affirm these positive affirmations aloud:*
God is stronger than the strongest.
God is my source.
God has a plan for my life.
God will bring good out of this bad situation.
God forgives me.
God is with me.
Nothing is impossible with God.

*Expect the best—and you will get it.*

*Jesus Christ is the great attitude transformer.* For the greatest change in attitude, come to know Jesus Christ as personal Lord and Savior. Sheryl Dintelman, a sixteen-year-old, is a different girl now than when she started at our drive-in church not quite two years ago. Her attitudes have been so transformed that she no longer looks to be a sad person but a happy, smiling person. Here is her testimony in a letter that I received a couple of days ago:

I love New Hope and all of its members so much. In fact, I've built the best part of my life on its very foundation. Through New Hope God has answered my questions about life.

Sure, I have problems tangled up with the delicate threads of my future. But you see, God already has all of that under control and I can be at peace with myself in knowing that.

If I had only known that joy would replace sadness, that confidence would be planted in place of fear, and love sown instead of suspicion, I would have given my life to Jesus Christ long before I did. But you see, that was the whole problem. I didn't know Jesus and therefore, I couldn't have known.

God has really changed my life. I guess I expected him to just "zap" my life into changing like I could snap my fingers. It didn't happen that way, though. It happened gradually, slowly—slowly enough that I had the joy of experiencing that change that God wanted me to make.

I just realized one day that I was happier, more grateful than I could ever remember being since I was a little girl. The storm and the lightning last night gave me a real feeling of closeness to God. I kept thinking of how small I felt next to that great Presence, like a little girl next to her father. I just knew that I didn't have to be afraid, that everything was under control. I knew then that nothing happens unless God wants it to happen. I kept thinking of the words "I made you and I will take care of you." The world really isn't that spooky when you know that God is bigger, is it? God bless.

Sincerely,
Sheryl Dintelman

Keep on keeping on. It takes not just one choice or two choices or three, but thousands of choices to become a positive-thinking person. Old habits do not die easily. New habits are established by great effort and persistence.

How do you eat an elephant? One bite at a time.
How do you climb a ladder? A rung at a time.
How do you cut down a tree? A chop at a time.
How do you become a positive person? A choice at a time.
Keep keeping on, choosing positive thoughts.

Like attracts like. Think positive thoughts and you send out positive vibrations; you activate the positive world around you. You gather friends who are positive thinkers. These friends will cause you to think more positively, and you will become a more positive person. Think positively and you'll get positive results.

A man becomes what he thinks. The Bible says, "For as he thinketh in his heart, so is he" (Proverbs 23:7). One of my very favorite pieces of literature is *The Great Stone Face* by Nathaniel Hawthorne. On the side of the mountain was the face. It was strong, kind, and honorable. Living nearby was a boy by the name of Ernest. Day by day he would look at that face, and he was thrilled by what he saw. Through his boyhood and even after he became a man, Ernest spent many hours gazing upon the face on the mountain.

There was a legend that some day a man would appear in the community who would look exactly like the face. For years that legend had persisted. One day, when the people were discussing the legend, someone suddenly cried out, "Behold, behold, Ernest is himself the likeness of the Great Stone Face." Indeed, he was. He had become like his thoughts. So you will become like your thoughts.

> *"Your attitude should be the kind that was shown us by Jesus Christ" (Philippians 2:5, TLB).*

A Christian friend of mine, Jerry Schmidt, works as a salesman for a newly formed sausage company. Recently, after work one night, the government inspector stopped Jerry and asked him why he was always so happy. Jerry smiled and said, "I'd be glad to tell you. I'm happy because Jesus Christ lives within me and is my personal Lord and Savior." The man smiled and said, "I thought so. Your attitude shows it."

What could be greater than to have the mind of Christ within? You, too, can have Christ's attitude within you.

# 7

# Love Again, Only More

What does our world need now? Rich in material things; broad in understanding; feasting off the results of a multitude of scientific discoveries—yet everyone agrees something is missing in our world today. It seems like the whole world is bent on destruction. In the midnight hour of our civilization, something stronger than the forces of destruction is needed. Something that can beat hate. Our world today desperately needs . . . love!

*What the world needs now . . . is love!*

Love is the medicine for the sickness of our world. "So faith, hope, love abide, these three; but the greatest of these is love" (1 Corinthians 13:13, RSV). As the Apostle Paul wrote these words under divine inspiration, there was no hesitation, no wavering, no hedging. This is the way it is. Love is central in God, and love can become central in man. There is nothing, absolutely nothing, that can take its place. Lack love and you lack being a complete person—no matter what else you have.

*There is no substitute for love.*

Who needs love? No one questions a child's need of love. Verified cases of homeless babies having been loved or ignored in hospitals during infancy prove without doubt that for normal emotional, mental, and physical growth, babies need loving care and affection. Children need to be loved into loving. Children are taught love by being loved. Parents need to receive love from their children. Grandpa and Grandma need to be loved. Employers and employees need to be loved. Friends need to be loved. Strangely enough, we clergymen need to be loved.

The broken need love—oh, how they need it! It is love in action they need, not platitudes or high-sounding words. There are times when giving love is merely being present, in silence, saying nothing, doing nothing, period. Before Jesus raised Lazarus (the beloved brother of his dear friends, Mary and Martha) from the dead, he first was with them weeping. Love joins—it never separates or sets apart. He did not preach to them about keeping their chins up. He wept and entered in as one of them. He participated.

> *Jesus gave his love to the broken. Jesus said, "They that be whole need not a physician, but they that are sick" (Matthew 9:12).*

*Please love me.* For weeks before my wife left me to never return, ironically I had been preaching a series on "How to Love." As it turned out, it was almost as if I had spent weeks before my life-shattering experience, preparing the congregation for this, and was asking them to love me in spite of my failure. My dozen years spent in the ministry had been filled with giving love to other people. I had gotten so much joy and personal fulfillment in giving to others, I had not even bothered to stop and feel my need to be loved.

Now, broken apart emotionally, I desperately, urgently, needed someone to love me. Someone to listen, someone to be concerned, someone to care. Most of all, someone to believe I was still, in spite of this divorce, a worthwhile person. Thousands of years before, the preacher in Ecclesiastes said, "Cast thy bread upon the waters: for thou shall find it after many days" (Ecclesiastes 11:1). The hours of love that I had given to others throughout my ministry were now given back to me in my time of greatest need.

How thankful I am for the Christian counselor who without charge and at great personal inconvenience to himself, listened to me by the hour, day after day and many times at night. He loved me by giving me his attentive ear. Then there were those who reached out to me and adopted me into their family when I was so very much alone and far away from any members of my own family. What a priceless love they gave to me.

During this time I felt all alone, whether I was with people or by myself. Hurting, hurting, I needed a good friend. It was a day never to forget when God brought into my life my best friend.

Her name was Margi, as those who know her best call her. She was a sixth grade teacher in one of the suburban community school systems. Her father had been a pastor for many years. In the years before we met, Margi's mother had passed away. This was a very difficult adjustment for her, to live without the close relationship she had enjoyed with her mother. So there was in this beautiful lady's life, as in mine, a great need for companionship and Christian friendship.

Near Margi's school was a Chinese restaurant that became our favorite meeting place after school each day. We would order a pot of tea and sit and share very warmly and deeply with one another. Amazingly, the very first time we ever talked together, we were at ease with one another. It has been our joy to communicate deep levels of feeling in ways which very few people ever have the privilege of sharing together. One of the greatest things we shared very early was our mutual desire to serve God with our lives. One thing I have never been able to get over was how Margi knew all about me in my brokenness, yet she loved me. To me, this is love. With each passing day, our friendship grew and as it did, there was born a love that was to never die.

Who needs love? *Everyone!* You need it, I need it. People are willing to go to the ends of the earth to find love. To be loved and wanted is a basic psychological need that surges in the heart of every human being. It is the "sweet mystery of life" and all the world is seeking it.

A man and wife visited an orphanage where they wanted to adopt a child. In an interview with the boy they wanted, they told him in glowing terms about the many things they could give him. To their amazement, the little fellow said, "If you have nothing to offer except a good home, clothes, toys, and the other things most kids have, I would just as soon stay here." "What on earth could you want besides those things?" the woman asked. "I just want someone to love me," replied the little boy. Isn't love what we all want?

*If you have love, you have everything.*

## WITHOUT LOVE, WE PERISH

Multitudes of persons today are sick in spirit. As human beings we not only become sick in body and in mind, but in spirit. There is a third dimension to human suffering that has not always been recognized, says Dr. Peter S. Ford, a family physician. Without love, that thoughtful and keen consideration of others, man is anything but well and healthy. Without love we perish.

Jealousy, envy, rage, anger, resentment, hate and all other similar negative emotions are disease-producing. They not only make others sick of us, but they make us sick inside. It is of interest to see that all these disease-producing emotions are concerned primarily with protecting and coddling the self. All these negative emotions could be summarized under one title—self-centeredness.

Centuries before modern psychiatry discovered that negative emotions cause many psychosomatic diseases, the Bible not only condemned them, but provided the cure. The antidote is love. Love is the one and only antidote which can save man from the many diseases produced by negative emotions. Without love —that thoughtfulness and keen consideration of others—man is likely to perish from a variety of diseases of mind and body. It's love or perish.

Without love, it is a pretty ugly scene. The phone rang in a high society Boston home. On the other end of the line was a son who had just returned from Viet Nam and was calling from California. His folks were the cocktail-circuit, party kind—drinking, wife-swapping, gambling, all the other things that go with it. The boy said to his mother, "I just called to tell you that I wanted to bring a buddy home with me." His mother said, "Sure, bring him along for a few days." "But, mother, there is something you need to know about this boy. One leg is gone, one arm's gone, one eye's gone, and his face is quite disfigured. Is it all right if I bring him home?"

His mother said, "Bring him home for just a few days." The son said, "You didn't understand me, mother. I want to bring him home to live with us." The mother began to make all kinds of excuses about embarrassment and what people would think . . . and the phone clicked.

A few hours later the police called from California to Boston.

The mother picked up the phone again. The police sergeant at the other end said, "We just found a boy with one arm, one leg, one eye, and a mangled face, who has just killed himself with a shot in the head. The identification papers on the body say he is your son."

Yes, when men live without love, the scene gets ugly. Our greatest need is for love. Without love we perish. God is Love. Without God we perish. You know this is true because you see it vividly illustrated before your very eyes every day. When men choose to live apart from God, a necessary ingredient is missing, and the results are one bad scene after another. Many try to live without love, without God, but the results are never very pretty. Without God—let's face it—we perish.

Good news . . . the greatest truth in your world . . . "For God so loved the world that he gave his only begotten Son, (to die for us), that whosoever believeth in him should not perish, but have everlasting life." In younger life I was thankful that God's love saved me from going to hell for eternity. Now after working with people and seeing the things people do to themselves and to each other, I am thankful we need not perish daily from all the negative diseases of mind and body. My friend, you don't have to be selfish and go on living with ills that kill you because "God so loved the world." God and his love can transform your world from hate to love.

*Love is the antidote—just what we need.*

Yesterday evening I arrived home, went into the bedroom to change my clothes, and happened to glance out the window. Two feet away from my window stood a young boy. Fifteen feet behind him stood huge blackberry bushes we had enjoyed eating from for the last couple of weeks. There, right in the middle of the bushes, on top of our picnic table, were two other kids, uninvited. These invaders had trespassed into our privacy. I opened the window and yelled at them to please leave and not pick blackberries anymore without our permission. They looked at me as if I were "Mr. Bad Guy," said some unrepeatable things, and finally made their way toward home. A few minutes later and they were back with their mother. The mother wanted to know why I had to be so hostile, and not let her children pick blackberries. After she left, I felt just terrible inside. I did not want to have bad feelings with our new neighbors. All these emotions, the strained relationship with the neighbor, were just eating me up inside.

I decided to do something about it. As Christ's follower, I was to be an example of love in action. I made my way across the field, and knocked on the door. The lady came to the door, and called her children. I took the opportunity to very kindly and very diplomatically explain to the mother, in front of her children, exactly what had happened as I saw it. I then concluded by saying: Friendship was more important than berries. I explained that I didn't really mind the children picking berries, it was their trespassing on our privacy I did not like, but I wanted to be their friend and I wanted them to be my friends. Then I smiled. As it ended up, the children apologized, I apologized, everybody felt good, everyone was friendly. Love won the day.

*Love wins again and again.*

Several years ago I arrived to preach special services at a church in Denver. On a Wednesday afternoon, during the series, I went with the pastor to visit a lady who had requested we come. Soon after we got seated, she dropped the bomb and announced she was going to ask her husband to get out. She wanted a divorce. Martha said, "I don't love Mike any more and that is that." As she continued talking, it was evident she was destroying their marriage with all the negative emotions she was holding onto on the inside. While Martha was talking with my pastor friend, I played with little Tommy. He was four, had big brown eyes, and was smart and just a lovable little boy. As we were departing from the home, little Tommy with pride in his eyes, said to his mother, "Daddy will be home pretty soon." When I heard this, I thought I would cry.

As I stood up to preach on Sunday morning, my passage of Scripture was, "For God so loved the world . . . we need not perish." There to my surprise sat Mike and Martha with little Tommy. That morning I shared how much we desperately needed God and his love to be healthy and happy, and to enjoy life's best. I told how "while we are yet sinners, Christ died for us. If we would receive Jesus as Lord into our life, he would transform us with his love." While I was talking, a miracle started happening.

At the conclusion of the message, I asked those who would receive Christ into their lives to come forward and stand for a prayer. Here came the couple whose marriage was dying from a lack of love; hand in hand they came.

As they prayed to God, who is the source of all love, a miracle happened. They discovered they could love. They need not go on perishing. Friend, with God—you need not perish. You, too, can love. I looked down when we finished a prayer of commitment and they had their arms around each other, tears streaming down their cheeks, and there was Tommy with the biggest smile you have ever seen.

It's love or perish—you decide.

## EVERYTHING IS BEAUTIFUL WHEN THERE IS LOVE

Everything is beautiful in its own way!

To an engineer the new bridge just being completed is beautiful.

To the scientist each new discovery is beautiful.

To the ecologist clean air to breathe is beautiful.

To the surgeon a successful operation is beautiful.

To the gardener flowers and shrubs are beautiful.

To the astronaut space is fantastically beautiful.

To the musician well-performed music is beautiful.

To the baseball fan a home run is beautiful.

Whoever you are, wherever you are the world over, the greatest, the most beautiful, is love!

God's love is the greatest:

It is without limit.

It is sufficient.

It is dependable.

It is continuous.

It sees beyond our ugly sin.

> Only a love like God's can bring the very best out of us.

*God's love can make the difference in your life!* Not tomorrow but now, starting right this moment. You don't have to live anymore with love lacking on your part. Receive him now, and let him fill you with his love.

Our love has become a beautiful love. Margi has given me so much love. On our third anniversary, she gave me a very special card and this is what it said:

I'm always finding reasons
For loving you still more—
Some words you say, some things you do
You haven't done before—
More reasons why my fondest dream
Is that each day may bless
The dearest husband in the world
With every happiness!

Then she added, in her own handwriting, these words: "Dale, these three years have been the three greatest years of my life. I'm looking forward to the fourth. You have changed my whole life and have brought me a world of happiness. Thank you! All my love, from the luckiest girl in the world! Me!"

*With God's help, your love can be as beautiful as you make it.*

## LOVE COMES ALIVE WHEN YOU GIVE IT AWAY

A baby's need for love is one-sided. His need is to receive love. Until a child has been loved into loving in return, the entire procedure is for him to receive. Here is the crux of the failure of adults to understand or practice love. When we think of our need for love, too often we think only in terms of how much we need someone else to love us as though we were still babies. We dwell on our need to be appreciated, respected, pampered a little, thanked. We think of how much we enjoy the attention of others. Here is where the great distortion occurs. We are just as much in need of giving love as we are of receiving it—perhaps even more.

A children's song says: "Love is something if you give it away, give it away, it's just like a magic penny. If you give it away, you end up having more."

I love the story of the little boy who moved into a new neighborhood. He was shy and quiet, and his name was Chad. One day he came home and said, "You know what, Mom? Valentine's Day is coming and I want to make a valentine for everyone in my class." His mother's heart sank and she thought, "Oh, how I wish he would not do that." Because every afternoon she would watch all the children coming home from school, and they would be laughing and hanging onto each other, books under their arms, all except Chad. He always walked behind them. But she thought she would go along with Chad. So glue, paper and crayons were purchased. For three weeks Chad painstakingly made thirty-five valentines.

When the day came to deliver the valentines, he was so excited! This was his day. He stacked those valentines under his arm and he ran out the door. His mother thought, "You know, this is going to be a tough day for Chad. I'm going to bake some warm cookies and give him some milk when he comes home from school and maybe that will ease the pain. He probably won't be getting very many valentines."

That afternoon she had the warm cookies and the milk out on the table. She went over to the window and scratched a little bit of the frost off the glass and looked out. Sure enough, here came the big gang of children, laughing, valentines under their arms. They had really done well. And there was Chad, coming up behind. He was walking faster than usual and she thought, "Bless his heart, he is ready to burst into tears. His arms are empty." He came in the house, and she said, "Darling, Mommy has some warm cookies and milk for you." But his face was all aglow. He just marched right by her and all he could say was, "I didn't forget a one—not a single one!"

*Life's greatest joy is to give your love away.*

*It isn't a song until it's sung. It isn't a bell until it's rung. It isn't love until it's given away.*

The late distinguished psychiatrist, Dr. Smiley Blanton, in his book with the telling title *Love or Perish,* shows that the more capable we are of responding to people in love, the healthier and happier we are.

God has created us to love. To love is to be happy. Your

wholeness depends on your entering into the lives of those around you, and giving your love away. Love is the only thing that can make a man give two hoots about another human being. Without this love, man loses all dignity and becomes a selfish animal, clawing for his own survival. Love is the greatest!

The only one who can stop you from loving is you! Too often we become "pot-bound." What does this mean? Recently my wife Margi had a plant which grew like a weed, but after a while it stagnated and began to look old and droopy. It had become "pot-bound." A cramped root (heart) changed beauty into ugliness

It is when we become stubborn, prejudiced and opinionated that we are "pot-bound." God wants to enlarge us, to free us, to love limitlessly. With God, there is no limit to love. You see, it's not our job to change people, it's our job to love them, to allow God to work through us with his love. Nothing has the power to change us like love. Do not allow yourself to be pot-bound. Open up your heart. Enlarge your love.

*Love can change the attitude.*

As you allow God's love to flow through you, and give that love to other people, you will once again believe in yourself and enjoy true self-love. There is no greater feeling than to be used of God. Believe it—God wants to use you to touch some other person who needs to feel loved.

God matches up touchers with those in need. A little seven-year-old, blue-eyed, blond girl knelt by her bed to talk to Jesus. An older sister, sitting on the other bed close by heard her pray, "Jesus, would you please touch me with your hand on top of my head?" All of a sudden someone reached out and touched the little girl. As the little girl finished her prayer and looked up, her big blue eyes were wide with wonder. After a while she grew a little suspicious and asked her older sister if she had been the one to touch her. The sister admitted she had. Little sister protested, "Why did you do that?" "Because," answered big sister, "God told me to reach out and touch you."

*When you give love away it helps others and it heals you.*

*The more we practice his love the better our lives become. A*

young man and woman deeply in love with each other have an unbeatable optimism; they think they can pay the bills whether they have the money or not. They think they are going to love, despite all the problems other people have found insurmountable. The facts are, if they could keep this unbeatable optimism, they probably would. As young couples begin to bump up against the problems of life, things begin to happen that cause their optimism to be leveled off at a low level of expectation. Problems funnel into dead end streets. The glory road of young marriage becomes a one way street of disappointment, filled with tired ruts. Why? Because the optimism born in love has been buried under the maze of life. The anniversaries are still observed but the spark is gone. They have stopped practicing their love.

I knew well a couple along in years who went through a severe tragedy. This crisis among other things involved financial disaster. Most people would have grown bitter. Filled with self-pity, they might have thought life had handed them something unfair. And had they taken this attitude, most people would have felt they were justified. But instead, they talked it over with each other and their friends. They said, "We still have our health and we still have each other. God is going to help us to overcome, and we will fight back, and we will gain the losses we have suffered." A spontaneous kind of optimism began to operate between them as their love generated the energy they needed to overcome their losses. Through this tragedy, they began the most useful period of their lives. The optimism which came through divine love gave their lives a thrust everyone could admire.

> *There is nothing you cannot overcome with his love.*

## MAKE LOVE YOUR HIGHEST AIM

*Let love lead.*

A salesman was far away from home, driving down an unfamiliar country highway. All of a sudden he came upon a barn which had a huge bull's-eye painted in the middle of it. He could hardly believe his eyes. There in the middle of the bull's-eye were hundreds of arrows. Every arrow was inside the bull's-eye. As he drove on down the highway, his curiosity got the best of him. He turned his car around and drove back to where the barn was, to take another look. Then he spotted a farmhouse close by. So he drove to where it was and met the farmer. After they got acquainted a little, he said, "Say, could you tell me who the excellent marksman is who shot all the arrows inside the bull's-eye?" The farmer almost laughed out loud, then he explained, "That was the work of the village idiot. The village idiot had come out and shot all the arrows at the side of the barn, and then climbed up there and painted the bull's-eye around all the arrows to create the false appearance that he was a great marksman."

We are like that so often in our lives. We do everything but truly practice love, all the time telling ourselves we are hitting the bull's-eye and all the time kidding ourselves.

All my life I have been a very goal-oriented person. My goals have helped me to achieve many things I could not have achieved otherwise. My lifetime goal has been to build a great church for the "unchurched thousands," a church with multiple ministries to thousands of people. To achieve this goal I have given my time, my energy, my money. Nothing has been too large or too small to give, in order to achieve this one great, driving goal. This, I believe, is a worthy goal. It is a great thing for God. If I achieve it in my lifetime, it will help thousands of people. It brings the best out in me. I believe it is God's will for my life. However, it is also where I failed most in my first marriage. My true confession is, it was having this goal as number one that was my point of failure in my previous marriage.

Whatever you achieve or accumulate, if you do not love, what do you have? There are a lot of good things one can do, but without love, what good is it?

My first goal, my highest goal, which makes my life so much more meaningful today than yesterday is love. No matter what you do, make love your highest aim.

*Number one goal—to love.*

The marriage Margi and I have together today is a tremendous success, because both of us are determined to make love our highest aim. It is this that fills our life with joy, with sharing, with enduring one another's shortcomings, with helping each other to overcome and become. My greatest delight is giving my love to my very best friend and wife, Margi.

There is nothing greater than love.

There is nothing stronger than love.

There is nothing more healing than love.

There is nothing more beautiful than love.

There is nothing more fulfilling than love!

With love not only *can* you win, but you *will* win

# 8

# Put Your Failures behind You and Move Ahead

I am a failure forever. Past achievements in the ministry do not matter now. Abilities, spiritual gifts God has given me do not make any difference, even though a large portion of my lifetime is ahead of me. The fact I love God with all my heart and want more than anything else to be used in his service does not seem to matter either. Any of the circumstances that brought the divorce about are not even considered. I am a divorced minister in the church I was brought up in, which brands me as a failure in the ministry. To the officials of my denomination, I am a washout with no way to ever return to a position of pastoring one of their churches. I understand there is nothing personal in this, that it is the blanket sentence passed on any minister whose home is broken by divorce.

To most churches of a conservative persuasion, a divorced minister is a failure, period. Today my heart bleeds for the multitudes of men who have been washed out of their churches. Who, yes, have failed, but worse yet, have been branded failures forever. The church of Jesus Christ must be more redemptive than this.

Having been brought up in a conservative evangelical denomination, there was nothing in the world more of a failure to me than divorce. It was bad enough what others thought, but the failure I felt inside myself was like a 300-pound weight, being carried on my shoulders everywhere I went. A sense of failure can wipe a man out. From my own experience, I want to share with you how to define failure in a positive way so it will help you instead of hurt you.

*Define failure in a new positive way.* Stop allowing negative thinking people to dictate to you their definition of failure. The negative thinker says:

Failure is a disgrace.

Failure occurs when one fails to achieve.

Failure is anyone who fails.

Failure is final and total.

All this is a gigantic falsehood—don't you believe the negative thinkers.

> *You were created for something greater than to live with a failure complex.*

## FOUR THINGS YOU NEED TO KNOW ABOUT FAILURE

1. *To fail is not to be a failure.* Because you have failed here and over here, and possibly in another place, do not allow yourself to believe you are a failure. You have simply failed at several different points in your life. Life is so much more than a few happenings.

*No person is a total failure.* When we center our attention on one failure, or a cluster of failures, it gets all out of proportion until we can't see anything else. But no one is ever a total failure. Every person I've ever met has something about his or her personality that is successful. Center your attention on your successes rather than your failures. It is displeasing to God for us to mope around over our failures. To do so is a denial of the power of God in our lives. As Christians we need to relinquish our failures to him, put them in his hands, then turn our attention on our successes and develop a success complex. When we do this, we can do so much more for Jesus Christ and his cause because success builds success.

2. *To err is human.* I wonder where we ever got it in our minds failure was a disgrace. This is one of the things we need to unlearn. If failure were a disgrace, we would all be disgraceful people, wouldn't we? Because the truth is, at some time every man has failed. The Bible says in Romans 3:23, "All have sinned, and

come short of the glory of God." Be patient with yourself. You are a human being who deserves to be treated with human kindness.

3. *No man is ever a failure who tries.* A young man eager to be on time for his first day of work walked hurriedly down the sidewalk. Right in front of a bench, where the village loafers were sitting, he stumbled over the seam of the sidewalk. As he stood up and brushed himself off amidst the roaring laughter of the loafers, he said, "Go ahead and laugh, you'll never fall, because you're never going anywhere."

*Failure is no disgrace when you've tried your best.*

*It is a crime to live without goals to reach for.* Without goals we have nothing to make us grow and expand. Those who drift through life not trying to better themselves, live boring lives. A man cannot respect himself until he gives himself to life. To withhold yourself is to lose all the way around. "I would rather attempt something great and fail, than to attempt nothing and succeed."[1] The Apostle Paul said it this way in the Bible, "I press toward the mark for the prize of the high calling of God in Christ Jesus" (Philippians 3:14).

*Life's greatest failure is to stop trying.*

4. *Failure need never be final.* Because a marriage relationship is bad now does not mean it needs to continue to fail. It simply means you have got to try harder. You have come to the place where you need to face up to some things. You and your mate can grow, communicate, come to greater understanding, and go on to rebuild something fine and beautiful together.

This is a new day. Because you failed in a past marriage does not mean you cannot succeed in a new marriage; because you lost a job yesterday does not mean you cannot succeed in a job today; because you failed in business in the past does not mean you cannot succeed now; because you failed the driver's test does not mean you cannot take it again and again until you pass it. Never allow yesterday's failures to wipe out the possibilities of tomorrow's successes.

[1]Robert H. Schuller, *Move Ahead with Possibility Thinking* (Garden City, N.Y.: Doubleday & Co. Inc., 1967), p. 159.

## WASH THE FEAR OF FAILURE
## OUT OF YOUR MIND

*Kill your fears before your fears kill you.*

No emotion paralyzes like the emotion of fear. It stops a salesman from calling on a prospect. It makes a young man about to pop the question to his love, hesitate. Fear causes a job hunter to give up before he asks for a job. This crippler of us all causes an executive, faced with a decision, to have cramps in the middle of his stomach. The fear of failure defeats many a man before he even gets started.

*Fear is far more destructive to personality than failure.*

*See your fear of failure for what it really is.* As my good friend and I shared together, the truth finally came out into the open. What was really eating away at him was not the fear of failure as he thought, but the big fear of what others would think if he failed. Well, his business venture did fail, and this is what he found out. People who he thought were his friends but deserted him because of his business failure were not really friends after all. A true friend is one who steps in when the whole world steps out. Happily, my friend discovered he had some of the best people in the world for his friends, because they stuck by him through it all. The best people in the world run to the side of an honest loser and ask, "What can I do to help?" It is wonderful to see your true friends.

Decide you would rather build your self-dignity than crawl in a hole and die. You have failed once, twice, maybe ten times, so what are you going to do? Give up, lose self-respect, and die of boredom? Never! For of all sad words of tongue and pen, the saddest are these: "It might have been." People who refuse to move ahead because they are afraid of failure do not protect their self-respect, they lose it. You were created for something greater—learn from your failure and move ahead!

*Remind yourself—there is no progress without risk.* Not until you experience failure can you be sure you aimed high enough. Low aim to me is the shame. Success is making the most of your God-given opportunities, while failure is failing to make the most of the gifts God offers you. The man who does things makes many mistakes, but he doesn't make the biggest mistake of all—doing nothing!

Because you've failed doesn't mean you're going to fail again. The truth is, your chance of success is now far greater. You now know many of the pitfalls that caused you to fail before and you can avoid them.

## PROFIT FROM YOUR MISTAKES AND MOVE AHEAD WITH NEW DETERMINATION

Beaten by his own failures, a young man dropped into my office chair. "What's the use," he said, "I am a failure. Once I had lots of hopes and plans. That's a laugh now. Everything I touch goes sour. I have flubbed everything with my stupid mistakes. Nobody will ever believe in me again." At age twenty-seven, he had just been fired from his job, because of a serious mistake he had made.

"Why did I do it?" he cried in emotional misery. "How will I ever explain this to my wife? I had the chance of a lifetime with this company. I have just blown the best opportunity I will ever have. Why did I do such a stupid thing? I am nothing but a dumb failure."

After the young man had given himself a good going over, I said to him, "John, there is no use crying over spilled milk. The only sensible thing as I see it is for us to analyze together your mistake and why you did it. Learn all you can from this mistake, then put it behind you, forget it and move ahead to do better in the future."

*Learn all you can from your mistakes.*

Yes, everyone makes mistakes. Two kinds of people I observe—those who learn from their mistakes and those who do not. Being a disciple means being a learner. A true disciple of Jesus is one who learns from his mistakes.

*Failings are opportunities to learn—to learn how to do things better the next time—to learn where the pitfalls are and how to avoid them.* I have learned so much more from my failings than I have from my successes. You, too, can learn the best lessons from your failures.

Gene was a rugged-looking man who had worked hard all his life. In his late teens and early twenties, he had worked as a coal miner in West Virginia. Now he worked as a plumber by trade. He was my neighbor and friend. He had at one time considered himself a Christian. Then something happened and he gave up. Now he was convinced if he were to become a Christian, he would fail.

On one occasion as we were sharing together about spiritual life, I asked Gene to read this from my Bible, "For by grace are ye saved through faith; and that not of yourselves: it is the gift of God: Not of works, lest any man should boast" (Ephesians 2:8, 9). When Gene finished reading, I asked him, "How will any man make it to heaven? What I mean, Gene, is there any way I could earn my own way there?" Gene smiled. He knew the Bible well enough to get the point. He said, "I guess if a man gets to heaven, it will be because of what Jesus did."

I looked my friend right in the face and said, "Gene, you are like so many others I have met who know being a Christian is by far the very best way to live. I imagine you really want to be a Christian, but you are afraid, afraid you will fail again. I want to let you in on a secret. Gene, if you commit yourself to Jesus Christ today and become a Christian, you will fail. You can expect to. How many times did your children fall before they learned to walk?"

"Oh, hundreds of times, I guess."

"Gene, didn't your children learn to walk because they learned from their falls and had a determination to keep on until they could walk? Well, spiritual life itself is likened to physical life. It starts with birth and moves gradually with months and years toward maturity. God wants to use even our failings to teach us to live his way."

No one is ever a failure in the Christian way until he decides to just give up and stop trying. At the moment of spiritual birth, God gives us the name Christian, then we have a lifetime to grow into this wonderful name.

We learn from our mistakes not to do some things. History records the story of Thomas A. Edison who in trying to develop a light bulb was unsuccessful in the first 6,000 experiments. One day when someone asked him if he was not discouraged, he said, "No, I am now well-informed on 6,000 ways you cannot do it."

Then came the day Thomas Edison successfully produced the light bulb. Without all those previous failings, we would still be in the dark. Many times, like Edison, we have to learn failure before we learn success.

Suppose someone offered to give you your choice between a very successful business, with several thousand dollars in the bank, or a struggling business with wisdom. Which one of the two would you take? A large majority of people mistakenly would reach for the money. Far more important than money is wisdom! With wisdom you can achieve many wonderful things. If you're fortunate enough to have the wisdom and experience, thank God for it—wisdom is worth more than money.

*Learn to use failures as stepping-stones.* As a young man, Abraham Lincoln ran for the Illinois legislature. He did everything possible to win his campaign, but was defeated by a landslide vote. Then he went into business with a partner. In spite of earnest efforts, the business failed, and Lincoln spent seventeen years paying up the debts of a worthless partner.

He fell deeply in love with a beautiful woman, only to lose her in death. Reentering the field of politics, he ran for Congress but was badly defeated. He tried to secure an appointment to United States Land Office but failed.

In 1856, he was a candidate for the office of Vice-President of the United States. Again defeated. In 1858, he was defeated by Douglas in the race for a seat in the Senate. In the face of defeat and failure, he rose to be elected President of the United States. You can learn to use failure as stepping-stones.

Here are eight miracle drugs for your emotional scars. They have helped others to put their past behind them and move ahead, and they will help you.

1. *Accept your own shortcomings.* Just think—if you were perfect, you would not have any friends. No one could relax with you, you wouldn't even belong to the human race. How do babies learn to walk? Trial and error. As they are learning, they stumble and fall. Do we call them a failure? Of course not! We recognize walking as a process.

Suppose you are on a new job, and there are many things about that job to learn. In the beginning days, any boss in his right mind does not expect you to perform that job with perfection. It takes time to learn how to do it. Every area of life is like this, it takes time to learn how to do it. When a couple get married, it takes quite a while to adjust and learn how to live together. The big thing is to be a learner.

*Nobody is perfect.*

2. *If you have sinned, admit it and start over again.* All the world loves an honest and truly repentant person. In the entire roster of great persons listed in the Holy Bible, only one man is called "a man after God's own heart." That man was David. Strangely enough, he committed the sins of murder and adultery, but he knew how to repent for his failures openly, honestly, and sincerely. In Psalm 51 are these unforgettable words, "A broken and a contrite heart, O God, thou will not despise" (verse 17).

We are to learn from our sins the truth that abundant life is not in that direction, but in a different direction where there is not sin. Did you ever wonder why God told all the details of sin in the Holy Bible? It is all there—you name it, and some characters in the Bible did it. Why did God put it all there? So you and I could learn that the wages of sin is death without personally having to go through the hell of it all. Wise indeed is the person who can learn from the failures and victories of others.

3. *Forgive your mistakes.* It's most important to forgive yourself. There is no way you can be happy if you're holding a grudge against yourself. Rub in the ointment of kindness, apply it gently in the areas where you hurt. Whatever you do, stop torturing yourself with self-blame.

*You are not the same person today you were yesterday.*[2]

4. *Forgive others.* People are people, they are not gods. They are just human beings like you and me.

5. *See anything that has happened as water under the bridge.* One of America's best loved preachers, Dr. Norman Vincent Peale, was given a story by his friend and editor, Grove Patterson, who first wrote this article in the *Toledo Blade,* under the heading, "Water Under the Bridge."

A boy a long time ago leaned against the railing of a

[2]Robert Schuller, *Self Love: The Dynamic Force of Success* (New York: Hawthorn Books, Inc., 1969), p. 131.

bridge and watched the current of the river below. A log, a bit of driftwood, a chip floated past. Again the surface of the river was smooth. But always, as it had for a hundred, perhaps a thousand, or even a million years, the water slipped by under the bridge. Sometimes the current went more swiftly and again quite slowly, but always the river flowed on under the bridge.

Watching the river that day, the boy made a discovery. It was not the discovery of a material thing, something he might put his hand on. He could not even see it. He had discovered an idea. Quite suddenly, and yet quietly, he knew everything in his life would some day pass under the bridge and be gone like the water.

The boy came to like those words, "water under the bridge." All his life thereafter, the idea served him well and carried him through. Although there were days and ways that were dark and not easy, always when he had made a mistake which couldn't be helped, or lost something that could never come again, the boy, now a man said, "It's water under the bridge." And he didn't worry unduly about his mistakes after that, and he certainly didn't let them get him down, because it was: Water under the bridge.

6. *Do not be controlled by what has happened to you—but be controlled by where you want to go from here.* Don't you do it—do not let your old hurts, defeats, setbacks hold you back. Some people experiencing emotional hurt say I'll never trust anyone again, I'll never go into business again, I'll never marry again. When you use those words *never again,* you're allowing past failings to move in and control you. Don't let the past run your life now. Don't allow yesterday's mistakes to wipe out this new day. What has happened has happened. So give it to God and let it go like water passing under the bridge.

Hank was talking to me about the death of his wife. It was normal for him to be grief-stricken. I tried to comfort him by telling him his wife was a beautiful Christian, and I was sure she was in Heaven. I soon saw this did not comfort him. I encouraged him to talk. He told me how a few days before her death, they had a violent argument and he said some very unkind things to her. And now this was on his mind and was all he could think of. Over and over again he heard the ugly words he said to the woman he loved. He was filled with guilt and haunted by his shameful words.

I said, "Friend, we all have things we would like to forget. God tells us in his Word exactly what we must do in a situation like this." We opened our Bible to Philippians 3:13 and I said to him, "Here is your prescription. 'This one thing I do, forgetting those things which are behind, and reaching forth unto those things which are before.'" We prayed together and as we did, my friend released his intolerable guilt into the hands of God.

> *Live in the present, not in the past. Look straight ahead, not in the rearview mirror.*
>
> *When God created you, he made no mistake.*

*7. Move ahead with determination.* An unforgettable character on the American scene in this century was Eddie Rickenbacker. His achievements in aviation will probably never be matched again. Eddie liked to say that the American's greatest freedom was the freedom to go broke, and he found out the hard way. The ace of aces in the air came home from war deciding he wanted to go into business for himself. He got some financial backers and manufactured a sporty car called the Rickenbacker. But unable to compete with big time automobile companies, Rickenbacker wound up $250,000 in debt. This did not dampen his spirits very much. He said failure was the greatest word in the English language. He declared that if you have the determination, you can come back from failure and succeed.

Determination—that's the big word. Eddie Rickenbacker, with determination, did it. He not only paid off his debts, but he raised close to another million dollars and bought the Indianapolis Speedway, which he made famous. Do you know what successful people have that others do not have? They are just ordinary people like everyone else, except for one thing. They have determination.

*8. Look to Jesus who never fails.* You know it makes all the difference in the world where we focus our attention. If you look for shadows, that's what you're going to see. If amidst the shadows, you can look for the sunlight, it's there. If you look to

Jesus, who is himself brightness and optimism and eternal hope, he'll be there. A dear friend of my mother's wrote a song entitled "Standing Somewhere in the Shadows You'll Find Jesus." Thank you, Jesus, for being there when I need you. In the midst of any failure you are experiencing, Jesus is there . . . he is never more than just a whisper of a prayer away from you.

*Let a winner lead your way—Jesus!*

Develop a strong personal faith in God. One of the boldest of American businessmen was the late Robert LeTourneau. He shared the secret of his daring in this simple thought: "God is my partner. How could you ever be afraid if you had a partner like that?"

God makes the difference in any situation. God is never victimized by circumstances. He is always the Master. Nothing is too hard for God.

Any man, with God, is a majority anywhere, anytime, in any situation. The man who has God may be down for the moment, but he is not beaten. With God you can bounce back stronger than ever. "If God be for us, who can be against us?" (Romans 8:31).

# 9

# Dream a New Dream

Give yourself a lift—hitch your wagon to a dream. Not just any dream, but a big dream. I believe in big dreams! When a person begins to dream big, he is actually beginning to think the way God intended men to think. Lee Braxton, Chairman of the Board at Oral Roberts University wrote me this: "We have a dream to build the best athletic program. We plan to win a national basketball championship, if not this year then the next, or however long it takes us to reach that goal. Our coach knows this and he is challenged to come up with a winning team. Also all our athletes know and share this goal. We at ORU have made known our goal for our Athletic Department. We look at this as a way to witness to forty million men who turn to the sports page first every morning in the newspaper."

*Dreams cost nothing.*

Two summers ago my wife Margi and I attended Dr. Robert Schuller's Institute for Successful Church Leadership in Garden Grove, California. We met people who had dared to dream some pretty fantastic dreams. One man I met, whom I judge to be in his sixties, had ten years previously become burdened for young single adults, and dared to dream a beautiful dream. Single young adults in most churches are left out, and yet their needs are unequalled by any other age group. His dream was to create an alive vital program to meet the needs of single young adults. Here was a man in his fifties without training, without experience, without funds, but with a beautiful dream of helping people who

**94**

had tremendous needs. He went to work, wholeheartedly giving himself completely to the fulfillment of the dream. Today there are hundreds of single young people involved in that great Christian single adult program. It all started with a layman who had a dream.

*You, too, can dream an enchanting dream.* You can begin a great project with no money, only a dream. God created the earth with—nothing! We can dream dreams and the bigger they are, the more our blood is stirred to accomplish—to have—to be—or to achieve. I dare you to hitch your wagon to a dream.

*Go ahead–let your imagination go.*

The long months following my father's death were sheer pain, grief, and loss for my mother. At sixty-nine years of age, when the man for whom you have lived your life is suddenly gone, what do you do? You go out in public and you feel like a lost soul in the middle of the crowd. You drive past a restaurant, and your heart is pricked with pain as you remember that this is the place you ate every Saturday night. At night in the big house you are alone, and you are afraid. How do you fill up all the endless hours? What do you do? How do you put it all together?

Two thousand and five hundred miles away, Margi and I did not know what we could do to help. We would call Mom each week and talk to her, but we felt so helpless. She seemed so full of gloom, despair, and loss. If it were not for her faith in God, I do not know how she would have made it through this time of brokenness. Mother had always been a very active person, and all the inactivity was killing her inch by inch.

Then a miracle started! I received a letter. In it Mother shared with me about a possible opportunity to form and direct a senior citizens' ministry in a large church in Mt. Vernon, Ohio, where she lives. For the first time since my father's passing, the letter had some hope, optimism and cheer in it. Mother wanted to know what I thought. I immediately wrote back and said: "Get involved. Dream a new dream."

At seventy years of age my mother's life has come alive again—because she has dreamed a new dream. What a difference in her letters, in her conversation, in her outlook. Her new dream has given her a new lease on life. Days are filled with planning, programming, directing the new Joy Club. J - O - Y, she tells me, stands for "Just Old Youth." Just a few months ago my mother hardly knew what to do with herself. Now she has more to do than she can get done in a day. This dear lady has a dream that lifts her, gets her up in the morning, causes her to plan into the night, helps her to serve people in a most satisfying way. Has your life been broken apart? Are you disappointed? Filled with depression? Then dream a new dream. The sooner the better.

*Need a miracle? Then dream a new dream.*

In my first pastorate, while going door to door looking for prospects for the Christian way, I first met George. This silver-haired man, age sixty, with tears streaming down his cheeks, shared with me the deep anguish of his heart. The failure of his first marriage twenty-five years before had kept him away from our denominational church, the church of his birth, for all of these years. Right or wrong, George was convinced in his mind that if he went to church he would be an outcast. That day as I prayed with George for Christ to come into his life, a dream was born within me that some day I would build a great church for the unchurched Georges, a place where the broken, the beaten, the turned off, people with their fears of organized religion, could come as they are and find new hope. New hope, like Jesus Christ himself, will never turn away any person. I have a dream! It is a beautiful dream!

I transplanted my dream into richer soil. For ten years I served as a pastor with a denomination. With each passing year came an increasing realization my opportunity to achieve my God-given dream for building an innovative church within the traditional structure of the church was very slim. Many men serve best within the framework of an established denomination, but with my particular personality, my greatest fulfillment was to come outside of a denomination. When my divorce wiped out my creditability with the denomination, it served to break me loose emotionally from the denominational fellowship I loved and forced me to transplant my dream into richer soil. By richer soil I mean a fellowship where people from a variety of backgrounds and economic levels could all come together in Christian love. A place where the barrier could be removed and I could see it big and keep it simple.

As a result of my own brokenness, my dream came into sharp focus. I was to pioneer a healing fellowship for the "unchurched thousands" where the broken could come and be healed, where the discouraged could come and be lifted, where those searching for love could come and receive Christ's love. New Hope Community Church, Oregon's first walk-in/drive-in church, is my lifetime dream in the process of being accomplished. Out of what once was nothing but a dream, God is healing hurting people. New Hope—my God-given dream for many.

You, too, can dream a magnificent dream. No matter who you are, or where you are, or what has happened to you, you can dream a new dream. Dreams are not for those who have achieved, but for those who want to achieve. Maybe you will dream like the woman I met just recently who had just been divorced, dreaming passionately some day she would meet a man, and together they would establish and build a Christian home.

Whatever you do—dream.

Dreams:
    Lift us,
    Inspire us,
    Put new zest into our lives,
    Motivate us and move us ahead,
    Help us to reach higher than ever.

> *Do something greater than you've ever done before.*

## YOU HAVE WHAT IT TAKES TO ACHIEVE A DREAM

You want to be somebody? Stand out from the crowd? Be remembered? Deep within all of our hearts there beats a secret desire: To be a somebody!

You've got it—yes, you do—you've got it! God gave it to you. To every person God gives certain abilities and talents. When God created you he gave you talents. Then he says: "If you use what you have, I will increase it, but if you do not use it, you will lose it."[1] Use it or lose it! It's up to you.

[1]Charlie "Tremendous" Jones, *Life Is Tremendous*, p. 28. Used by permission.

Our world is full of unused talent and abilities. Gold is where it is dug up and discovered—it is there all the time.

You've got it, so:

Dig it up. Discover it. Develop it.
Use it before you lose it!

*Use it.*

One of the best stories I have heard about the difference between using it and not using it was first told in *Guideposts* magazine by one of my favorite writers, Dr. Norman Vincent Peale:

A college boy on the football team was the number one goof-off. He liked to hear the cheers, but not to charge the line. He liked to wear the suit, but not to practice. He did not like to put himself out. One day the players were doing fifty laps, and this showpiece was doing his usual five. The coach came over and said, "Hey kid, here is a telegram for you." The kid said, "Read it for me, Coach." He was so lazy he did not even like to read. The coach opened it up and read, "Dear son, your father is dead. Come home immediately." The coach swallowed hard. He said, "Take the rest of the week off." He didn't care if he took the rest of the year off.

Well, funny thing, game time came on Friday and here come the teams rushing out on the field, and lo and behold the last kid out was the goof-off. No sooner did the gun sound than the kid said, "Coach, can I play today? Can I play?" The coach thought, "Kid, you're not playing today. This is homecoming. This is the big game. We need every real guy we have, and you are not one of them." Every time the coach turned around, the kid badgered him: "Coach, please let me play. Coach, I have got to play."

The first quarter ended with the score lopsided against the coach and his team. At half time, they were still further behind. The second half started, and things got progressively worse. The coach, mumbling to himself, began writing out his resignation, and up came the kid. "Coach, Coach, let me play, please!" The coach looked at the scoreboard. "All right," he said, "get in there, kid. You can't hurt anything now."

No sooner did the kid hit the field than his team exploded. He ran, blocked, and tackled like a star. The electricity leaped to the team. The score evened up. In the closing seconds of the game, this kid intercepted a pass and ran all the way for the winning touchdown!

The stands broke loose. The kid was everybody's hero. Such cheering you never heard. Finally the excitement subsided and the coach got over to the kid and said, "I never saw anything like that. What in the world happened to you out there?" He said, "Coach, you know my dad died last week." "Yes," he said, "I read you the telegram." "Well, Coach," he said, "my dad was blind. And today was the first day he ever saw me play."[2]

God is not blind. He watches to see what we do with what he has given us. Open your eyes to what you can do!

You say, I don't have any talents! and I say to you, That is not true! Maybe you have yet to discover your talent. Maybe you have put it on the shelf. But believe me, you have got it.

*Use it or lose it.* Our universe is built on this principle. There are hundreds of examples of the "use or lose" principle in Nature. In certain caves in Newfoundland there are fish which have lived for so long without light, although they have eyes, the eyes no longer see. Naturalists tell us long ago both the kiwi of New Zealand and the emu of Australia were capable of flying, but from long disuse, their wings have now reached such a point they are useless. Many of you know from painful experience what happens to muscles that are not used. Did you ever go to a picnic and play ball after you hadn't used those particular muscles for a long time? Use it or lose it.

A salesman was really using all his abilities and he was reaping great success in sales. Then he began to coast, not using what he had, and he was losing. There is no room for coasting—use it or lose. Some churches are full of coasters, as are some companies. It is little wonder they are losing. Use or lose.

Jesus said, "Unto every one which hath shall be given; and from him that hath not, even that he hath shall be taken away from him" (Luke 19:26). With God, it is use or lose.

All of spiritual life is based on this principle—use or lose. Use prayer and your spiritual power increases. Neglect prayer and for you, the joy of prayer dies.

Take the love God gives to us, his children. Give it away—use

Charlie "Tremendous" Jones, *Life Is Tremendous,* pp. 62-64. Used by permission.

it—it will increase. Hoard it—hold onto it—and you will lose it. Use it or lose it—you decide.

*Dream a dream that will make you dig–discover and develop what you have.*

Dream a dream big enough to make you stretch, go beyond, use all the abilities and talents God has given you. To use what you have is to discover, to develop. And when you do, you will become the beautiful person God created you to be. While it is true you have within you the ability to achieve—untapped resources, potential beyond what you think—in order to realize all of this, you need a big dream.

*It takes an all-consuming dream to bring the best out of a man.*

*All achieving begins with a dream.* In 1973, O.J. Simpson, one of the most exciting runners in football history, broke the professional football record for total number of yards gained by one individual player. In an on-the-spot interview following the record-breaking game, O.J. shared who it was that had inspired him to achieve this dream. As a Black, growing up on the streets of Los Angeles, he idolized another all-time great Black football player by the name of Jim Brown. Jim Brown was at one time the long-time record holder of the most yards gained in professional football.

One day at the age of thirteen, O.J. saw his hero eating ice cream in a famous ice cream parlour. The skinny kid walked up to his hero and announced, "Some day, Jim Brown, I am going to break your record." And that is exactly what O.J. Simpson achieved.

You, too, can be an achiever. Make New Hope's Achiever's Creed yours:

Whatever the mind can conceive
and I will dare to believe,
with God's help, I can achieve.

*For every person alive, there is more than one big dream.*

Take five steps to assure that your dream will come true:

1. *Dream a worthwhile dream*. If you don't have a dream, it is impossible for your dream to come true. There is no force in this world as powerful as a dream. Jesus had the greatest of dreams—to seek and save us all. His entire life was given to the pursuit of the fulfillment of this all-consuming dream. No other man has even come close to making the impact for good on the world that Jesus made—the man with the greatest dream.

> *People are attracted to the man with the big dream.*

*A dream begins with an idea.* Recently I was sharing with our church's banker my dreams concerning the development of New Hope Community Church. With great enthusiasm I was telling about the wonderful things that were happening in people's lives through this God-given ministry. With great discouragement, he told me about all the money problems his church was having. After he had finished with his tale of woe, I looked at my banker friend and said, "I have never seen a church yet that had money problems—only idea problems. Let your church get some great ideas, get a vision, and you will attract wonderful people to help fulfil those dreams. Great people are just waiting to give money to an idea that fulfils a vital human need.

> *A need-fulfilling idea is of far more value than money.*

*Select only the most worthwhile dream.* Some people spend their lives dreaming dreams that aren't worth much. I remember a young man whom I counseled a few years ago who spent lots of time dreaming about how he was going to win the next door neighbor's wife and make her his wife. Needless to say, his dream turned into a nightmare. His dream did not have any lasting value.

When a dream-inspiring idea comes into your mind, ask yourself three questions: (1) Would this be a great thing for God? (2) Would it help hurting people? In other words, does it serve people? (3) Would it bring the best out of me? If the answer is yes to all three of these questions, then you have the making for a worthwhile dream. Before embarking on the greatest adventure of my life, the launching of New Hope Community Church, these three questions were the test I put to myself. When the answer was in the affirmative to all three, I moved ahead with the assurance this was God's will for my life. What could be greater than to do something wonderful for God, help a lot of hurting people, and develop and bring the very best out of myself?

Watch out—do not ask, "Would this be the easy way?" "Would this be cheap?" "Would this be secure?" "Would it be without obstacles?" I don't know how it ever got started in Christian circles, but there seems to be wide acceptance of the false thinking that if it is the will of God, then suddenly all the doors will open and there won't be any obstacles. Nothing could be further from the truth!

How tragic! How awful to realize that New Hope came so close to never being. Where would the hundreds of people be whose lives have been lifted and changed in the first two years of this ministry? What about the thousands of unchurched New Hope will give new hope to in the years ahead? If I had killed my God-given dream there would be no New Hope. Someone has said that hell would be God showing us what could have been accomplished if only we had dared to move ahead with a positive idea.

I hate to confess it, but I almost killed New Hope before it was born. You say, Didn't God give you a beautiful dream to build a "church for the unchurched thousands"? A place where people from all backgrounds could come and be lifted with faith, hope and love? Yes, all my life it seemed God had been giving me this dream. What a beautiful dream! But do you know that at the last moment I almost killed my dream? Why? Because there were obstacles, big giant obstacles! They stood like insurmountable mountains before me.

Obstacle 1: We would lose all our friends. Obstacle 2: We would be leaving the church of our birth. Obstacle 3: My preacher father whom I loved and respected didn't understand, and thought I was making a mistake. Obstacle 4: A little thing you might have heard of called money—it costs no money to dream, but it does cost to live. Obstacle 5: The unknown, the uncertainty of it all—what if we fail? As we gave our attention to the obstacles, we were being defeated.

It was only when we got our eyes on the God-given opportunities instead of the obstacles that we were able to make up our minds to say, "Yes, Lord" and move ahead. As my good friend, Dr. Schuller says:

*No one has the power to kill your dream but you.*

2. *Draw the plans.* You can't build a skyscraper without a plan, and you can't expect to fulfil a dream without a lot of planning. I know a man who is always dreaming dreams, but that is the end of it. Unfortunately, I have never known him to formulate a plan of how to fulfil any of his dreams. We have all watched a person seize a dream and immediately go off half-cocked without proper groundwork and planning. The results are always messy and not very rewarding. The older I get, the more time I am spending in planning, and consequently my percentage of successful projects has risen to a high achievement level.

*To fail to plan is to plan to fail.*[3]

During the twelve months prior to starting our exciting venture, Margi and I were planning ahead financially. Soon after we were married, we cut up all of our credit cards and proceeded to work diligently at paying off completely both of our accumulated obligations. Six months before we started the new ministry, I advertised and sold our car, which I loved to drive but was anything but economical. In its place we bought an economy car which gave us thirty-two miles per gallon. In this one financial move we cut our living expense by more than one hundred dollars per month. Before beginning New Hope we sold our house in order to have all our earthly assets to put into our beautiful dream. How did we live for six months without a paycheck? By planning well in advance.

*One cannot expect to fulfil a dream without planning–planning–planning.*

3. *Dedicate yourself to fulfilling the dream.* The best dream can never be fulfilled without personal sacrifice. One day a young man came to Jesus, wanting to have eternal life, a wonderful

[3]Robert Schuller, *You Can Become The Person You Want to Be* (New York: Hawthorn Books, Inc., 1973), p. 24.

dream. Jesus told him he could have it if he was willing to give it all he had. The young man was unwilling to pay the price and he went away sorrowfully. Many never achieve their dreams because they are unwilling to give everything they have to fulfil the dream.

*There is no feast without a sacrifice.*

One does not fulfil a dream by wishful thinking. Achieving the dream comes through great effort and hard work. God is not going to do for you something you can do for yourself. Split the word *triumph* and you have *tri-umph*. It takes a lot of trying and a whole lot of umph, plus old-fashioned hard work to achieve success.

*The difference between the chump and the champ*
*is in the all-out effort.*

The greatest achievers I have ever known have all been *dedicated*—dedicated first to God, then to serving their fellow man, and to making full use of their potential to achieve. Years ago my father gave me a simple little formula for living a full and useful life. He said, "Son, do everything you are given to do like the success of it depends upon you. Then trust God like it all depends upon him."

A young energetic insurance man, Jim Grigg, shared with me the experience of hearing a man from Texas speak. The man had achieved the distinction of having sold 7,000,000 life insurance policies in one year. This was accomplished in spite of the fact that the go-getter lived in a town of 300 people in Texas. The successful man stood up and told the people he had been able to achieve this because: Number 1—God was his source. Number 2—He wanted to help other people . Number 3—He wanted to make full use of what God had given him. "Seek ye first the kingdom of God, and his righteousness; and all these things shall be added unto you" (Matthew 6:33).

You, too, can achieve the greatest of dreams. Dedicate yourself and all your aspirations to Jesus Christ. He is the inspiration and the motivation for all truly great achievements.

Let's do something great for God. I want to do something great for God with the life I have.

I would rather attempt something great for God than to have material security.

I would rather attempt something great for God than to have the approval of men.

I would rather attempt something great for God than fail to use what he has given me.

I would rather attempt something great for God than to be bored with life.

*To move ahead you must become willing to take the risk.* Look at the turtle! Until he ventures out of his shell and sticks his neck out, he is going nowhere. Want to move ahead to greater things? Then you have got to get out of your shell. People who win the prize are those who first stick their necks out. There are some wonderful achievements awaiting you, when you dare to move ahead with courage.

To me faith is calculated risk. It is having an idea, gathering all the available data. And if it is a good idea, a need-filling idea, a beautiful idea, and if the doing of it is within your power, then move ahead with courage and do it.

Why are we so afraid of failure? Since we started Portland's first drive-in church, several have said to me that before I started, they thought about what a good idea a drive-in church would be. A good idea? It is a great idea! Why didn't anyone do it before we did? Others dreamed about it and talked about it. But they were unwilling to run the risk. Faith is putting a good idea into action. Because we have taken this calculated risk and have gone ahead with what we believed was a great thing for God, we are seeing great spiritual miracles. We think as we continue to venture in faith that the best is yet to come.

You see, I have come to the place in my life where I would rather attempt to do something great for God and risk failure, than to do nothing and succeed! It makes a great deal of difference whom we are trying to please with our lives.

Jesus teaches us to dare. To the disciples who had fished all night and caught no fish, Jesus said, "Launch out into the deep" (Luke 5:4). Only when they put faith into action did the miraculous miracle of nets running over with fish happen. To the man with the withered hand Jesus said, "Stretch out your hand." He stretched it out, and his hand was restored. You want to be an achiever? Then launch out—reach out—dare to do it.

4. *Decide to get started.* Make a decision. Set a time to start! In

one recent year, the laymen of New Hope branched out into eight new home Bible study groups. Without exception, each of the leaders was apprehensive about getting started. I had to encourage each of them to set a time when they would have their first gathering. Once they set a date, they were off and running full steam ahead to achieve an alive Bible Study Fellowship.

*Stop making excuses for not starting.* Procrastination is your greatest enemy. Delay will turn pregnant opportunities into hollow possibilities. If you don't have the courage to move ahead now—accepting God's invitation to abundant living—don't be surprised if God gives that invitation to someone else. How sad to look back and to have to say, "It might have been me."

Our world is full of people who dream but never do anything. Step out from the crowd. Do something. Write a letter. Make a call. Get going. The hardest part of any job is getting started. So get the hardest part out of the way now! Begin.

5. *Determine to fulfil your dream.* If you try to achieve, you can count on some rough times. Discouragement will pound at your door, shouting, "Give up—give up—give up!"

If you are facing a trying time in your business, your marriage, your private, public, personal or professional life, and you are ready to throw in the towel . . . hold on! "Be of good cheer," Jesus said, "I have overcome the world" (John 16:33).

*Be determined.* If what you are trying to achieve is worthwhile, then it is worth the price. For everything worthwhile achieving, there is a price to be paid. Remember—there is no victory without a price.

Jesus is our example of determination. The humanness in him did not want to die the cruel, unjust death of crucifixion any more than you or I. The devil tried to get him to take another way out. His closest disciples tried to persuade him to not take the road of suffering for our sins. Jesus refused to be sidetracked. He counted the cost—said we were worth it—and set his face to go to Jerusalem to die for our sins. Aren't we glad he was determined? If what you are trying to achieve is great, then never give up.

*If it is worthwhile achieving, never give up.*

What should you do if it is a good idea but you do not think you are able to do it? Try it anyway. Just because you lack talent, ability, training, or money does not give you the right to say "no" to a good idea. It simply means you need a power greater than you—*you need God's power.* Whatever the mind can conceive and you will dare to believe—with God you can achieve.

Go forward with a big God. God gives his people a promise for the impossible. "It is the Lord who goes before you; he will be with you, he will not fail you or forsake you; do not fear or be dismayed" (Deuteronomy 31:8, RSV). "If God be for us (and he is) then who can be against us?" "I can do all things through Christ which strengtheneth me."

With God you can do it—I know you can. If it is the right thing to do, it can be done—and to think God has given you the idea. You are the one to do it—so decide now—make up your mind and move ahead.

# 10

# Turn Your Scars into Stars

This title was coined by Dr. Robert Schuller and has become a source of inspiration not only to myself but to thousands.

Friday afternoon, December 14, 1973, eleven days before Christmas, our church, New Hope, was struck a heavy blow. Without any advance warning and with no apparent reason, we were given notice by the management of the 82nd Drive-In Theater that our services would be terminated the following Sunday. Just thirteen months before, we had launched our ministry to reach "the unchurched thousands" in this theater. Our drive-in church had been an overwhelming success. Already we were reaching hundreds of people who had not been attending church previously. As I read the letter, my eyes focused on these heart-breaking words:

> This letter is to notify you that we do not wish to continue our premises for your use for church services as of January 1, 1974. It has been nice knowing you.

What a smashing blow to our new ministry! Are we going to lose a large part of the people who are coming to our drive-in service? Is this going to demoralize the dedicated workers we have? We were right in the middle of our winter season, and a move to another drive-in theater at this time could be devastating.

What would we do? Would we cry about being mistreated? No! Would we argue over the decision? No! Would we be beaten? No!

Would we retreat into a smaller ministry? No! Would we give up? No! Never!

Still shaken by the blow, I asked God to give me his answer. Friday afternoon God's Spirit planted the answer in my mind in the form of an idea. We would do something bigger and greater for God.

We would open up immediately our first morning walk-in service. Arrangements were made within a day to secure one of the new spacious theater facilities in our area to launch this new venture, a facility which would cost a million dollars if we had to build it. Besides, we would plan ahead and as spring came we would open up our drive-in service in a new outdoor theater. As it worked out, the 82nd Drive-in Theater, unknown to us, was being sold to new management. Within three months we not only had the new walk-in service in the morning, but were back in the 82nd Drive-in Theater, going stronger than ever. At New Hope, with God's help, we turned every scar into a bright star.

When life tumbles in, what then?

What does a person do when:

He finds out a teen-age son is on drugs.

He is told his sixteen year old daughter is pregnant without a husband.

A friend turns against him.

He is given a bum deal.

His wife tells him she doesn't love him.

The doctor says his sickness is incurable.

He loses his life savings.

He finds himself financially bankrupt.

He is without a job.

Someone he loves dies.

He blows his witness by losing his cool.

Someone hurts him deeply.

All these shattering experiences, and many more, happen in people's lives. Never a day passes but what someone, somewhere, is dealt a smashing blow. It is easy to pass off others' misfortunes, but when it happens to you, you feel it. It hurts!

A man who had just lost his job in the vocation for which he had trained for years, whose wife had left him, and who was facing financial ruin, asked me, "Pastor, what do you do when life tumbles in on you?" I said to this wounded and bewildered man, "I know what you are feeling. A few years ago my world tumbled in on me, and I felt completely beaten." Here is what I told this friend to do:

1. *Don't panic.* All is not lost. It only seems that way. The last chapter has not yet been written. It is never as bad in the long run as it appears to be now.

2. *Don't fight it.* Accept what you cannot change. Hearing of our dismissal from the drive-in, Marie, one of the employees, asked me if I had tried to write to find out why we had been asked to remove our services from the 82nd Drive-In. My answer was, "No, I don't want to waste creative energy. The big thing is, where do we go from here?" I have known people who spend their lives fighting unchangeable things. What a waste!

3. *Don't indulge yourself in self-pity;* you cannot afford self-pity. Self-pity is harmful. Like acid, it will eat away at your personality, filling you with gloom and despair. It will mar your relationship with others. It causes you to be resentful toward God himself. Nothing good has come into your life through self-pity.

4. *Don't hold onto ill feelings toward others.* Hang onto hurts and you hurt no one but yourself. I am not responsible for anyone else's actions or attitudes. But I am responsible for my own actions and attitudes. No one can break your spirit but you. Let God heal your broken heart.

5. *Don't keep rebelling.* Let's face the truth; life is not always just and fair. The most mistreated person in all of history was the kindest—his name is Jesus. As he was unjustly tortured to death, there was a final gasp and he was gone. The Roman commander in charge of the execution turned away. Converted on the spot, he was overheard saying, "Certainly this man was innocent" (Luke 23:47, RSV). When you don't understand it, do what Jesus did: "Father, into thy hands I commit my spirit" (Luke 23:46, RSV).

6. *Remember, because Jesus lives, no situation is hopeless.* God's day ends with the morning. There comes into almost every life a dark night, and it is so easy to feel it is the end, it will always be dark. But tragedy is never the final word. In Christ we have hope; no matter how bad things are today, there's always a better tomorrow. No matter what happens to you in life, no matter what

disappointments come, no matter what dreams are dashed, when you have Christ, you have hope. You have hope that:

> After the night comes a new day,
> After winter, a new spring,
> After the storm, a sun,
> After sin comes forgiveness,
> After defeat, another chance.[1]

## MANY HAVE TURNED THEIR SCARS INTO STARS

Easter Sunday morning, 1974, was New Hope's second Easter! For weeks we had prepared for this triumphant Sunday. Three thousand dollars had been invested in direct mail, newspaper, and television advertising. What an inspiring moment when I stood to preach the Easter message. First I saw the green hillsides, then just beyond, snowcapped Mt. Hood towering in the sky as if reaching to Heaven. There in front of me hundreds of cars were filled with joyful Easter worshipers. In my mind there flashed for a moment a scene three and a half years before when I was lying on a beach, broken, crying out of desperation, "Where the hell are you, God?" Now I was standing, preaching faith, hope and love to more people than I had ever preached to thus far in my life. I could not hold back the tears of joy as I said:

"Jesus! . . . . . I am sure glad . . . . . you're alive!"

> Because he lives—I can face tomorrow.
> Because he lives—all fear is gone.
> Because I know—he holds the future.
> And life is worth the living—
> Just because he lives.[2]

Bill Gaither

> *Because he lives you, too, can turn your scars into stars.*

---

[1]Robert H. Schuller, *Move Ahead with Possibility Thinking* (Garden City, N.Y.: Doubleday & Co., Inc., 1967), p.152.
[2]From "Because He Lives," © 1971 by William J. Gaither. Used by permission.

Glen Cunningham, the first of the famous American mile runners is a leader among overcomers. Glen was born on a Kansas farm. He attended school in a one-room frame building. The building was heated by a big stove in the center of the room. Glen and his brother were responsible for starting a fire each morning. One morning they came as usual to build the fire. Carelessly they poured kerosene in the stove, trying to hurry the process of fire-lighting. Unknown to the two boys there was still a live coal from the day before in the ashes, and a horrible explosion occurred. Glen made a mad dash for the door, and as he paused to look back, he saw his brother lying on the floor in front of the stove. Instinctively, Glen made his way back through the smoke and dragged his brother from the fire and smoke to the outside of the building. Tragically, a few days later the brother died, and Glen's legs were left charred and damaged by the flames. The family doctor was convinced young Glen would never walk again. Certainly no one dared to dream he would grow up to be a record-breaking track star.

Before the accident, Glen and his brother had already make up their minds to break the world record in running. Glen's disappointment and grief after the accident were painful. For days he was confined to bed, but eventually he was able to lean on the plow and hobble across the fields behind a mule. What determination he had! At the age of eighteen he intentionally got a job working on the loading platform of a Kansas City packing house. Although he could not walk too well, and could run very little, he could hobble in his own way at a very fast pace. He got the job at the packing house so he could build up the muscles in his legs.

Glen had an all-consuming passion to be a great runner. He would not give up his dream. In his early twenties he entered college. Here he put forth not only effort but extra effort—grueling hours, practicing, pushing himself further and further in preparation to become the track star he dreamed of becoming. At twenty-five years of age, with a pair of legs still scarred from the accident at age seven, still unable to walk very well, Glen Cunningham broke the world's record for the mile race, at a time slightly over four minutes. That wasn't enough. Two years later, he broke his own record. Glen Cunningham, with determination, turned his scars into stars.

A couple of years ago Art Linkletter, of television fame, was heartbroken by the tragic death of his eighteen-year-old daughter from an overdose of drugs. Some of you parents know what it is to have your heart broken by a child. Since that disastrous day, Art Linkletter has helped thousands of parents and kids to understand and beat the drug drag. With God's help this brokenhearted father is turning his scars into stars.

> *Overcome or overcomer—which do you choose to be?*

Let me tell you about an active fifteen-year-old high school athlete from the State of Indiana who dived into a pond and broke his neck. Fortunately he was pulled out of the water still alive, but unfortunately he has been unable to walk since the accident. Gerald Nees, at fifteen years of age, is confined to a wheelchair, probably for the rest of his life.

In a situation like this, it would be so easy to give up, be defeated, wallow around in gloom and despair—but not Gerald. He was not made of weak stuff. He was determined to turn his scars into stars. The first thing he decided to do was to graduate from high school. He just needed one credit to complete the requirements. He told his mother he wanted to take an art course. "But how on earth can you do that?" she asked. "Your hands cannot move." Determined, he showed her how he could draw with a pencil between his teeth. She encouraged him to take the course, and the new dream was begun for Gerald.

Becoming intensely interested in art, Gerald was granted an art scholarship by the University of Minnesota. Then came the day he received a scholarship from the Famous Artists School in Connecticut, where he learned to work with oils. Now in his thirties, Gerald Nees enterprisingly paints the things of beauty he sees all around him, holding a brush steadily in his mouth. He makes good money for his paintings and helps to support his family, who live on a fifty-acre farm. His paintings inspire and lift all those who are fortunate enough to see them. He has a love for life that is depicted in his scenic paintings. Gerald Nees is a member of the overcomers—turning his scars into stars.

> *When crisis comes, activate the spiritual resources God has given you—turn your scars into stars.*

Jesus turned his scars into stars. To Jesus:

Sorrow was his opportunity to compassionately share.

Adversity was his opportunity to advance.

Tragedy was his opportunity to triumph.

Personal abuse was his opportunity to show a persistent attitude of love.

*"With his stripes we are healed" (Isaiah 53:5).*

*Go on the offensive and do something to turn scars into stars.*

*Never settle for defeat.* You were created for something so much greater than to be defeated. It's God's will for you to be an overcomer, not to be overcome. With Christ's help you can gain a victory. You can find your way out of any difficulty. The secret is this: Never think defeat, never admit defeat, never settle for defeat. Make up your mind that you are not going to be defeated.

The book of Hebrews in the New Testament addresses itself to people who are having a difficult time. In the eleventh chapter the author calls the roll of a large number of persons who have become overcomers. They have succeeded in spite of fiery trials. He says, "Considering what these witnesses experienced, take heart in your present circumstances." In other words, they did it, they overcame, and so can you. Friend, you have just what it takes as much as anyone else does. Others overcome, and you can, too.

*No man can be defeated who will not allow it.*

People today are defeated for a variety of reasons. At the top of the list is the fact that they have no commitments. A man who is not committed to anything has nothing to live for. Every man needs something that captures his imagination and challenges him to keep reaching, to overcome, to go beyond. Royce, the philosopher, once said, "Unless you can find some sort of loyalty, you will not find unity and peace in your active life." The secret of a man's being is not only to live but to have something to live for. Jesus Christ not only gives a man something, but something worthwhile to live for. He leads a cause that calls for our best. A commitment to Jesus Christ and his cause lifts life like nothing else above the ordinary into the realm of the extraordinary. *A man committed to Jesus Christ can never be defeated.*

Firmly fix in your mind that you are going to live for Jesus Christ, no matter what else happens in your life. You, for one, are going to be committed to Christ's teachings and ways, whatever others do. Like the wedding ceremony—for better, for worse, for richer, for poorer, in sickness, or in health—I am going to follow Jesus. At Youth Camp when I was a teen, we used to sing, "I am determined, I've made up my mind, I'll serve the Lord." There is no way that a man who has made up his mind to follow Jesus can be defeated. Why? Because to follow Christ is to follow victory. *There is victory in Jesus.*

*Remember, there is no growth without struggle.* The way of struggle is the path that an individual must follow to expand, develop, progress, and become the person God created him to be. In everyone's life there comes hardship. That hardship becomes either an ordeal or a magnificent experience through which the individual becomes more like Christ. It is God's way of building and developing Christ-like spirit and character within us. There is no other way to be refined into a person of beauty.

> *Strength, both physical and spiritual, is the product of struggle.*

A sixth grade boy made it his hobby to collect cocoons and store them in his attic. Each day after school he would make his way to the attic to observe the cocoons that he collected. Under his watchful eye one day, the miracle of life unfolded. The newly formed butterfly was struggling with intense difficulty to break out of its shell and complete its metamorphosis. First it opened up a little hole, and then it took the struggler hours to enlarge the hole and at last emerge through it into the world. Soon, however, the newborn butterfly fluttered its wings and flew off into the morning breeze. The boy thought he had a bright idea. He would save the others from such a struggle. When the next one was trying to emerge from its shell, he cut a large hole so it could come through quickly into the new world. Not having gone through the hours of struggle, the weakened butterfly never gained the strength to fly as it was intended to fly. It is the struggles that give us strength to fly higher, to become what God created us to be.

> *There are powers within you that you can only discover through struggles and hardship.*

*When the going gets tough, the tough get going.* On the First Anniversary Sunday at our drive-in church, to our dismay we found that someone leaving the theater the night before had rammed one of the sound posts and caused the sound system to short out. Here we were, our First Anniversary Sunday, with no way to get any sound out on the field. Ironically, the topic of the sermon was: "Trying Times Are Times to Triumph." What do you do when you face a tough situation? One thing you do—you don't let your feelings decide for you. If I had done what I felt like doing, I would have packed up and gone home and said, "I'll see you all next Sunday." I asked the ushers to gather all the people in as close as they could, and I made full use of the public address system God gave to me. What an opportunity to not only tell, but show people how to turn scars into stars. Some said I preached better than ever, and they had gotten the message loud and clear.

*Look for the striking opportunity in each adversity.* Booker T. Washington used to speak of "advantages of a disadvantage." Booker was a great example of this in his own life. He was born a slave, and one of his jobs was to carry the books of the white children when they went to school. He personally had no books and was not permitted inside the schoolhouse. This man, who was a slave, would not be denied. He developed a strong passion for an education. While he was carrying those books, he would take full advantage and look inside them every opportunity he got. He did so much with the little that was given him. He later became one of the best educated men of his day. He became one of the great leaders as he devoted his life to making education possible for other members of his race.

*Every adversity hides a possibility.* [3]

One of the cities in the east was undergoing redevelopment in the downtown area due to an urban renewal project. There was an enterprising man who operated a store in the area for a number of years. It not only was a grocery store, but a general store, carrying many different items that people needed. In order to redevelop the area, bulldozers came in and leveled the area all around the store,

[3]Robert Schuller, *Move Ahead with Possibility Thinking* (Garden City, N.Y.: Doubleday & Co., Inc., 1967), p.75.

but left it standing there. Then they constructed a beautiful super-market on his right side, covering half a block. Then a gigantic discount house was built on his left side, where people could buy just about anything.

Here he was, right in the middle of these two super giants. What would he do? Would he be beaten? Would he give up? In the midst of what others saw as unbeatable adversity, this man saw his golden opportunity. He took most of his savings, went to the finest sign company in town, and had them make for him a magnificent, multicolored, neon-lighted sign, and constructed it right over the top of his little store. This is what it said: "Main entrance here." Every adversity is your opportunity to do something.

> *Every time one door closes, another door opens.*[4]

> *"If God be for us, who can be against us?"*

*Do something greater than you've ever done before.* I can speak from personal experience, because truly I am doing greater things today than I have ever done before. This is why my scars are being turned into stars. Use your imagination. Expand your mind. Consult an expert. Come up with a great idea, something greater than you've ever attempted before. And move ahead until, with God's help, you turn your scars into stars.

> *God created you to be a star in your own right, fulfilling your own God-given potential.*

[4]*Ibid.*, p. 73.

# 11

# Believe the Best Is Yet to Come

The most fantastic things happen to people who believe. No less of an authority than Jesus Christ himself says you do not have to be defeated. You can overcome illness, you can overcome weakness, you can overcome sin, you can overcome heartbreak, you can overcome failure. There is nothing or no situation you cannot overcome if you will believe.

Belief can change what appears to be an impossible situation. Belief unlocks the door to power beyond our own imagination. All things are possible—only believe. Jesus said: "If thou canst believe, all things are possible to him that believeth" (Mark 9:23).

Belief is:

The magic that lights up one's life with possibilities.

The initiator of all achieving.

The hook-up to a power greater than we are.

Every one of us needs to be believed in. It is amazing what having someone believe in you does for your self-image! One day Andrew brought his brother Simon to Christ. Carefully the Lord sized him up. He saw in him certain weaknesses, but he also saw possibilities. So Christ said to him, "Thou art Simon the son of Jona: thou shalt be called Cephas, which is by interpretation, A stone" (John 1:42). He was saying, "You are one thing now, but I see in you possibilities of being something else. I believe in you." We know at times the Lord's faith in Peter was severely tried, yet he kept on believing in him and eventually Peter became the man Jesus believed he could be.

A mother shared with me out of her broken heart concerning her son who was always in some kind of trouble. Time and time again this boy had broken his mother's heart. She came to me wanting to know what she could do to help her son get out of all the difficulty he was in. I said to her, "It looks to me like you have done everything a mother can do." Then I thought of the most important thing a mother could do for her son and added, "Just keep on believing in him." One of the greatest acts of love you can give to another person is to keep on believing in him, even when others have given up.

*Jesus believes you are a dream that can come true.* Someone has said that in the company of sinners Jesus dreamed of saints. To one who had missed the way he said, "Neither do I condemn thee, go and sin no more." Jesus did not minimize her sin, but neither did he fail to see her tremendous possibilities even as he saw her shameful past; he saw the possibilities of a new beginning and a better future, and this is what he chose to focus his attention on.

*God believes in you, now believe in yourself.*

*All things are possible if you believe in God.* Believing in the New Testament means receiving Jesus Christ into your life as Savior and Lord. Everything good starts with a decision to believe Jesus Christ and invite him to come into your heart.

You want an unbeatable life? Believe in Jesus.

You want to be a child of God? Believe in Jesus.

You want to overcome defeat? Believe in Jesus.

You want to have a better life? Believe in Jesus.

You want to beat defeating selfishness? Believe in Jesus.

You want to eventually win? Believe and totally dedicate yourself to Jesus.

God has a plan for your life. Finding and following God's plan for your life is the soundest, surest way to self-confidence. There is no greater feeling than to be in right relationship with God. If you are not in right relationship, you can be—starting now.

Believe wholeheartedly in God—and for you life will become unbeatable. Make this the dominating thought of your mind —God and I together are undefeatable.

Throughout the morning I had been working very diligently in my study on this book. Noon came and so I decided to take a lunch break. As I came out of my office I heard Jim Bisel and my secretary talking in the next room. He had two of his six children with him. I could tell these two little girls loved their daddy very much by the special sparkle that was in their eyes. Jim's ministry is to make people happy. He does Christian entertainment in rest homes and hospitals. He had come to our office so he could use the mimeograph machine to run off a special sheet to be used in a promotional program with which he was working with one of the local business firms. Jim and I chatted together a little while, and as I started to walk out the door, before I knew it, Jim and his two little girls were singing a song for me, called "Side by Side," with great big smiles written all over their faces. Before I knew it, we were all laughing and enjoying ourselves.

As Jim was leaving, I walked on out to the door with him. Just before he went out the door he rather casually said, "By the way, you might pray a little special prayer for us this week. On Monday we had an accident and our car looks like an accordian; on Tuesday when I went to work I discovered I didn't have a job any more; on Wednesday the County Tax Department phoned to say we owed some taxes from four years back, and if we don't get these paid in ten days, they'll come out and auction off our home."

All the time Jim was telling about these enormous problems, he still had his warm friendly smile that glowed all over his face—so much so, it took a few minutes for me to respond to the fact he really had some pressing problems that I needed to help lift up in prayer.

My friend smiled again and said, "Have a good day, Pastor," and he was off to another nursing home where he and the girls were going to put on another program to make people happy. You see, Jim is a man who has faith, hope and love. If you ask him why he is happy, he would tell you it is Jesus Christ who inspires him to smile and laugh.

As a result his faith has now grown until no matter what blow hits him, he has that overcoming power that just keeps on smiling and moving ahead.

*With God's help you can get on top of anything.* "I can do all things through Christ which strengtheneth me" (Philippians 4:13).

Only believe! The word belief is symbolic of a power that has no limitations within reason, and we find evidence of its influence wherever we find people who have achieved success in any calling.

*They conquer who believe they can.*

A few months ago, the television was on in our home and my wife Margi was surprised to hear our Achiever's Creed over the evening news. Channel 8 here in Portland was doing a news story on a lady who is an employee at a bus company. Her job is to answer the phone all day and take people's comments and complaints. Now this is one job I am sure I do not want—to have to listen to complaining people all day long. But because this lady had done such a great job of being warm and friendly in the midst of some pretty difficult conversations, the news had singled her out for honor in a news story. In the midst of the filmed conversation, the reporter asked her how she kept her cool with people who were usually upset. This charming lady simply pointed to New Hope's Achiever's Creed, hanging on her wall and read it aloud:

Whatever the mind can conceive
and I will dare to believe,
with God's help, I can achieve.

*Faith in God can move a mighty mountain.*

## NEVER STOP BELIEVING

*Lay hold of the power to persevere.* To achieve, to overcome, to win the prize, one must lay hold of the power to persevere. God's Word says, "Let us run with perseverance the race that is set before us" (Hebrews 12:1, RSV). Those who come out on top are those who stick with it through thick and thin.

The Bible constantly admonishes us to develop a steadfastness that is unmovable, always abounding and going forward toward the goal. There is no place for a quitter in the band of those who would live to win.

*Quitters never win. Winners never quit.*

History tells us the average speed of the Mayflower during the voyage across the Atlantic was just two miles per hour. That was slow enough to discourage even the most seasoned sailor, yet that voyage is remembered today as a glorious example of what persistence can achieve. There is almost nothing persistence cannot achieve in time.

> *Anything worthwhile is worth taking the time to achieve.*

*Be willing to take the time to achieve your goals.* If you are like me, you are impatient. Allow yourself to get impatient and you get all tensed up. We must remind ourselves: Anything worthwhile takes a while. The more worthy a goal is, the longer you can afford to work at it before it is achieved. The question is: Is this a worthy project? If so, then "let us not be weary in well doing: for in due season we shall reap, if we faint not" (Galatians 6:9). In the Bible and written in the universe is "the undeniable law of sowing and reaping."

The greatest man who ever lived, who had the greatest mission to achieve, had to wait. Though Jesus was anxious to get started to see results, to make it happen, for thirty long years he waited before he began his public ministry.

Instead of being out preaching the good news of the Kingdom, he sawed planks and hammered nails in a carpenter shop. Such a menial task for the Son of God to be doing! But as one studies the life of Jesus, he's made to realize that all the waiting was a part of his important preparation. The opportunities of his limited "today" became the stones out of which he built his eternal kingdom tomorrow.

Waiting is a hard thing to do. We're all children of the instamatic age, the now generation. Waiting through the difficult times is God's way of preparing us for better things to come. James writes, "Dear brothers, is your life full of difficulties and temptations? Then be happy, for when the way is rough, your patience has a chance to grow. So let it grow, and don't try to squirm out of your problems. For when your patience is finally in full bloom, then you will be ready for anything, strong in character, full and complete" (James 1: 2-4, TLB). What finer point is there to be developed in our Christ-like character than patience.

> *Patience is faith pushed to its farthest degree.*

Are you facing a difficult time in your life? Don't stop believing, don't give up. Practice patience—know that time can make all the difference in your world. Somehow we must discover that time can be put to work for the good of those who love God, and learn to practice patience. Do this, and with the passing of months and years you will find solutions to seemingly impossible problems.

*God's timing is perfect.*

I have had absolutely miraculous answers to prayer in my personal life. There was the time when I had just finished college and was making the tragic mistake of taking the pastorate of a little struggling church instead of going on to seminary. Then a friend phoned unexpectedly from miles away and came and took me 700 miles to a convention in Kansas City.

As long as I live I will be grateful for what happened there. On a Sunday afternoon, having asked God to direct my future, I walked from the hotel to the convention hall where there were twenty thousand people. As I stepped in the front door I ran head-on into the president of the local seminary. Without even saying hello, he said, "Dale, I will see you in seminary in a few days." I said, "Yes, Lord," and packed up and went to seminary. God's timing was just right. The years have shown how crucial it was for me to attend seminary at that time in my life.

God has never promised to give us exactly what we asked for when we ask for it. Two years ago Màrgi and I had our house up for sale, preparing to use our resources to start New Hope. How impatient I became as the days passed so slowly without a sale —April, May, June, July, no sale. I thought, Where is God in all this? Then just at God's perfect timing it sold. Not a day too soon or a day too late. A few days later we left to attend Dr. Schuller's Institute for Successful Church Leadership in Garden Grove, California. At the end of August, when we returned, the house deal closed immediately and we moved into an apartment in southeast Portland and launched the ministry of New Hope. As Dr. Schuller told us at the Institute: "God's delays are not God's denials."

*Be patient–believe–God is working everything out.*

*No man is ever beaten until he loses his patience.*

*Great men just will not be stopped.* My Grandfather Galloway was a man with that kind of determination. As I was growing up, Grandpa Galloway would come from Arizona to visit us in the summer time. On several occasions the camp meeting that my dad directed would be in progress. Invariably the people would ask for Grandpa to sing. Up in years, his voice would crack, and I am sure he would not win any music contests, but he would look up into the heavens and sing the favorite song he had written, and somehow when he sang, heaven came closer to earth. Appropriately enough the title of his own song was, "You Can't Stop Me." As I remember it, here's how Grandpa wrote it and sung it:

> I have many precious loved ones who have gone on
>   before,
> They are resting and waiting for me there;
> I'll be ready and watching when the summons comes,
> And that beautiful city we will share.
> You can't stop me, you can't stop me,
> I hear the voices calling o'er the sea;
> I'll make it to that city through Calvary;
> I feel his cleansing power and you can't stop me.
> O. V. Galloway.

You, too, can join the nonstoppers headed for greater things, reaching beyond to the heavens.

*Believe and never give up.*

## THE BEST IS YET TO COME

*Always keep hope going.*

Recently I heard someone say another person was hopeless. Something inside of me cried out, That's not right. To my mind the most profane word in the English language is not a four-letter word, but the word "hopeless." To say a person is hopeless, or a situation is hopeless, is a direct denial of the power of God. In Psalm 42:5, we read this powerful statement: "Hope thou in God."

*No man can live long without hope.* Psychiatrists have discovered no matter how deeply a person is depressed, no matter how despondent, if somehow they can inject a ray of hope in a person's mind, he will begin to recover. There was a time in my life where some people said, "There's no hope for him." They were talking about me. But because Jesus Christ is alive, I still held on to hope. I refused to believe them. And now I am the useful pastor of a great, growing church.

Many a person in our society today feels hopeless for one reason or another. Never before in the history of the world have people been so beaten psychologically. It is our unwavering belief that in Jesus Christ we have hope that all failure, all sins are forgiven. Now that biblical word *hope* is not something you wish for or dream of, but it is the assurance of the fact that God keeps his word.

God promises us that if we confess our sins, he is faithful and just to forgive us our sins. Good news: No one has to be beaten down by his sins another day. If you are beaten by your sins, your failures, confess them all to God and he will forgive you of every wrongdoing. I have never yet met a person that is hopeless. If you are alive, there is hope—there is Jesus!

If I could give to a man only one thing, I would give him hope. The kind of hope the Psalmist wrote about when he said: "For in thee, O Lord, do I hope" (Psalm 38:15). Hope in God is the only firm basis for achieving worthwhile aspirations.

*A man who has hope can never be defeated.*

What a difference between believing God causes tragic things to happen, and believing God allows them to happen. I, for one, do not believe God causes tragedy to come into our lives. God is not the author of evil; Satan is. A loving God permits incidents to occur for our own development and character.

When they first manufactured golf balls, they made the covers smooth. A certain young man, who was having severe financial difficulties, loved to play golf. He did not let the fact that he had only one old, beat up golf ball, keep him from playing. The men he was playing golf with had new, smooth, shiny golf balls. As they played, it was discovered Pete's ball got a lot more distance and went straighter than the smooth balls. Today all golf balls are manufactured with dimples all over the covers. With these rough spots, the ball goes further. So it is with life. It takes some rough spots in your life to make you go the farthest, to bring the best out in you.

> *A man who has hope knows that God will bring something good out of bad.*

I know an inspiring man of great faith who owned a lumber mill. Two summers ago, it was my privilege to be given a personal tour of this fascinating operation by the head man himself. Afterward he shared his tremendous faith in God with me as he related this experience:

In 1965, his mill was completely wiped out by fire. Only twenty percent of it was insured. From all appearances everything he and his family had worked a lifetime to build was wiped out.

Just before the fire, another small mill he owned, which had not been doing very well, had been put up for sale. A few days after the fire in the large mill, the small mill was sold. He took the money from the sale and insurance money, worked with his crews day and night for eighty straight days, and completely rebuilt the mill. Before the fire, lumber prices were a minimum of $48.00 per 1,000, to break even. However, in building the new plant, with many innovations and the best up-to-date machinery, the cost of the operation was reduced greatly. Just as the mill was completed, the price of lumber dipped to an all-time low and stayed there for the next year. If he had been operating the old mill, he would have lost $120,000 a month. But since the new mill was in operation, he was able to weather the storm. The next year, lumber rose to an all-time high. With tears in his eyes, he praised God and testified to the fact his Heavenly Father was taking care of him all the time.

My friend believes Romans 8:28, "And we know that all things work together for good to them that love God, to them who are the called according to his purpose." Here is the secret of true optimism—no matter what happens, God reigns, and he is at work to bring out good from bad. For the Christian, the best is yet to come.

One of my church members and friends had been in the hospital more than a dozen times during the past year. He and his family had been through so much I wondered how they could take any more. Now he was back in the hospital again, on the critical list, in the intensive care, cardiac section.

The morning after I went to visit him, his wife phoned. She said, "What in the world did you say to Glenn?" I said, "Well, I don't know, why?" "Well, before you went to see him yesterday he was so depressed and despondent. After you left, he was cheerful, at peace, and told me that if anything happened and he didn't make it, it would be all right, not to grieve, he would be well taken care of. He had a smile on his face."

After his wife hung up, I remembered what I had said to Glenn. I had quoted a few great faith-hope verses from the Bible and told him about a recent miracle of healing. Then I did something I had never done before. I said, "Glenn, look at it this way. When you know the Lord, as you do, the best is yet to come. If God heals you, that's going to be a whole lot better and if he doesn't, then you are going to go to Heaven and what could be better?" So I looked my friend right in the face and said, "Glenn, for you, the best is yet to come." And in that moment, Christian hope came alive. Wow! What a difference hope makes.

Since starting New Hope Community Church two years ago, we have been looking for the piece of land where we will fulfil our dream for building Oregon's first walk-in/drive-in church. The seven men who serve on our Board of Directors and myself have spent many hours in formulating the requirements for the piece of property we will purchase. The ten-acre plus spot must have accessibility to major freeways and visibility to passing traffic, must excel in natural beauty, and must be within fifteen minutes by car of one hundred thousand people plus.

After months of diligent searching, researching, and viewing, we found what we believe to be a beautiful spot, with perfect access to all the city's freeway systems.

Having used our God-given minds, we concluded that this spot not only met all our requirements but excelled in every point. We bowed our heads to ask God to guide in our decision-making. Talk about faith—here's a group of eight men deciding on whether or not to buy a piece of property that costs over $100,000, when they don't have even the money for the down payment. As each one of the men was praying and seeking God's will in this, God gave me New Hope's promise. Here it is:

Behold, I have set before thee an open door, and no man can shut it (Revelation 3:8).

Believing, we all said yes. This would be a great thing for God; it would help a lot of hurting people; it would pull the very best out of all of us. Believing we claim that marvelous scenic piece of property upon which to fulfil our God-given dream. You, too, have an open door before you.

To you God has given:

Healing for all your hurts.

Insights to build a better life.

Love to give away.

New dreams to dare you to reach beyond where you have been.

Obstacles to overcome.

Scars to turn into stars.

To you God has given: possibilities unlimited.

For you the sky is the limit. What matters is not where you have been—but where you are going.

Believe it—never stop believing, the best is yet to come!

Larry Mittler
4-27-82

( 9:30 Sun. Am.)